More Praise for *The Normal Bar*

"*The Normal Bar* is chock-full of good insights and findings in all areas of relationships, from sex and handholding to commitment and pre-nups. Over 100,000 respondents from around the world answered the authors' uniquely comprehensive web-based survey, providing a window into what's 'normal' when it comes to romantic relationships. Impressive research and results!"

—TERRI ORBUCH, PhD, bestselling author of *Finding Love Again*

"Are couples who fall in love at first sight happy decades later? What are the top desires of people in unhappy relationships? Is it normal to stop kissing in a long-term marriage? In *The Normal Bar* we learn fascinating bits about other people's relationship attitudes, behavior, and longings—and tips we can put into action to make our own relationships better."

—JOAN PRICE, author of *Naked at Our Age: Talking Out Loud about Senior Sex*

"Money? Sex? Deep dark secrets? If you wonder how your relationship compares with the rest of the world, *The Normal Bar* offers you a comprehensive heads up—most important, it suggests that growing healthier and happier may not be mission impossible."

—GINA OGDEN, PhD, LMFT, author of *The Return of Desire, The Heart & Soul of Sex,* and *Women Who Love Sex*

"*The Normal Bar* is an innovative, easy-to-read book filled with novel findings about relationships and helpful suggestions on making relationships better. I will use the important findings from *The Normal Bar* in my classes, in my papers, and in my clinical work."

—HOWARD J. MARKMAN, PhD, author of *Fighting for Your Marriage*

"*The Normal Bar* is more than a collection of surprising information—it's one of the most insightful guides to building happier, healthier relationships that I've ever read. I was encouraged and comforted by the authors' findings. Simply terrific."

—MARCI SHIMOFF, *New York Times* bestselling author of *Happy for No Reason* and coauthor of *Chicken Soup for the Woman's Soul*

"Facts trump opinions every time, and there are an amazing number of surprising facts in this book. Thanks to the authors' survey—which takes a quantum leap beyond any relationship survey ever undertaken—*The Normal Bar* marks a turning point in relationship advice books. In my thirty years as a professional student of romantic relationships, this is the only book that's actually taught me something new."

—GREG GODEK, author of the national bestseller *1001 Ways to Be Romantic*

"This outstanding book draws on thousands of surveys to find out what makes couples happy. Besides being entertaining and edifying, *The Normal Bar* can actually help most couples improve their relationships."

—BARBARA RESKIN, past president of the American Sociological Association

"A fascinating international compendium on women, men, sex, and love that—thank goodness—busts some entrenched myths about men. In the book you'll learn whether simple things such as reading to your partner can build deep intimacy, and whether date nights, compliments, and laughter can truly keep love alive. You'll also learn about 'pet names' and public displays of affection, and whether they spark romance. This book is scholarly, humorous and wise; above all, it gives superb advice. Indeed, after reading *The Normal Bar*, you'll have no excuse if your partnership isn't a dream come true."

—HELEN FISHER, professor of anthropology at Rutgers University and author of *Why We Love: The Nature and Chemistry of Romantic Love*

The Normal Bar

THE SURPRISING SECRETS OF HAPPY COUPLES AND WHAT THEY REVEAL ABOUT CREATING A NEW NORMAL IN *YOUR* RELATIONSHIP

Chrisanna Northrup

Pepper Schwartz, PhD

James Witte, PhD

HARMONY

BOOKS · NEW YORK

All rights reserved.
Published in the United States by Harmony Books,
an imprint of the Crown Publishing Group,
a division of Random House LLC,
a Penguin Random House Company, New York.
www.crownpublishing.com

Harmony Books is a registered trademark, and the Circle colophon
is a trademark of Random House LLC.

Originally published in hardcover in the United States
by Harmony an imprint of the Crown Publishing Group,
a division of Random House LLC, New York, in 2013.

Library of Congress cataloging-in-publication data
is available upon request.

ISBN 978-0-307-95164-9
eBook ISBN 978-0-307-95165-6

Printed in the United States of America

BOOK DESIGN BY BARBARA STURMAN
ILLUSTRATIONS BY STACY D'AGUIAR
COVER DESIGN BY MICHAEL NAGIN

2   4   6   8   10   9   7   5   3   1

First Paperback Edition

Contents

Acknowledgments

From Chrisanna Northrup

The Normal Bar concept and book would have never existed without endless love and support from my husband, Mark. Sweetheart, thank you for entertaining the kids and taking care of the house so that I'd have the opportunity to pursue my dream. You've been such a trooper through this whole journey, and I couldn't have done it without you.

To my kids, Jake, Shelby, and Luke, thank you for sitting with me patiently for hours while I wrote and for not giving me a hard time when I'd say, "It's almost done," knowing I was nowhere near done.

Stacy D'Aguiar, thank you for bringing all my visions to life!

Thanks to Joseph Castagnola, who has always supported my creative passion and has had to listen to my nonsense day in and day out.

Thanks to Elisa Esparza who always managed to keep my stress level down by stepping right into my shoes and taking over my day-job responsibilities on a moment's notice.

And thanks to my dear friend Kristine Grigsby, who was my on-the-fly editor and sounding board.

Glenn Bautista, you saved me a couple times, not sure what I'd do without you.

And thanks to Helen Zimmermann, our agent, who from the moment I pitched her this book idea never let me go.

From Pepper Schwartz

I want to thank Fred Kaseburg and my children, Cooper and Ryder, for their support.

FROM JAMES WITTE

Thanks to Connie, Jonny, Victoria, Aaron, Heidi. Our love for each other is a very good normal.

AND FROM ALL OF US

Thanks to our editor, Rick Horgan, and to our publisher, Tina Constable, for the opportunity and for making this happen.

A special thanks to Roy Pargas, codeveloper of OnQ. Without Roy's able assistance we wouldn't have been able to collect the survey data that is the basis for *The Normal Bar.*

A big thanks to Peggy Northrup and her team at *Reader's Digest*—we're forever grateful for all of your support.

Thanks to our other media partners—Huffington Post, AOL, and AARP—from whom we gathered more data than we ever could have imagined.

Thanks to all the people who helped ensure our success either by directly supporting us or by saying "yes" to working with us: Arianna Huffington, Sara Wilson, Willow Bay, Jennifer Barrett, Mary Hickey, Beth Domingo, Raimo Moysa, Keller Felt, Megan Baker, Barbara O'Dair, Seth Grossman, Lorna Davis, Deb Colitti, Ingrid Arna, Yang Yang, Linda Sivertsen, and Ariane de Bonvoisin.

And, finally, thanks to the tens of thousands of people worldwide who participated in our survey and shared their intimate personal stories with us. This is our gift back to you. Enjoy!

The Normal Bar

The Genesis of the Normal Bar

The Normal Bar was conceived during a relationship crisis that became an opportunity for marital rebirth. My husband, Mark, and I had been together for well over a decade when we started to question whether we were as happy as we could be in our relationship. At the time we were both so busy with work, the house, and our three kids that we barely had any energy left for ourselves, much less for each other. I remember thinking, is this as good as it gets? Curious to know if this was normal, I asked some of my closest friends, who also had been married for over ten years, how they felt about their relationships. I was stunned to learn how many of them were struggling. One of my friends confided that she hadn't made love to her husband for six months. Six months! I thought, there's no way that could be good. But who was I to judge? Mark and I had our own laundry list of relationship issues, and I knew the normal that we'd created for our marriage was making us both more miserable than we cared to admit. Was this the price *everyone* paid for working full-time while raising kids? That was too depressing a thought to accept without further inquiry. I had to believe there were *some* long-married couples whose normal made them happy! If

I could find them, then maybe Mark and I could learn from them what we needed to do to create a better normal for ourselves.

But how would I find them? Like a lot of women, I equated relationship happiness with those dreamy scenes you see in movies—you know, the ones where the guy sweeps his true love off her feet and tells her he loves her so much he can't live without her, then proves it with endless, incredible sex. Unfortunately, much as I wanted this vision to be true, I had a sneaking suspicion it wasn't very realistic. Deep down, I knew I needed to find some "real" people who were happy in their relationships—if such couples even existed. What did their sex lives look like? How did they sustain that feeling of being in love decade after decade? What were their secrets for keeping sex satisfying over the long haul? What were their tricks for maintaining trust and openness, for avoiding—or surviving—arguments? How did they manage to remain playful, affectionate, deeply connected, and romantic even with kids, family, friends, and work constantly competing for attention? If I could gather up all these secrets and insights about what actually works and what doesn't, then Mark and I could lay out some guidelines and begin to reshape our own relationship.

The information I was seeking wasn't available in any books, Web sites, or other media resources I could find at the time, so it seemed that the only way to learn from happy couples would be to track them down myself and put my questions to them directly. Fortunately, Mark endorsed this project, for it soon took on a life of its own.

I began by reaching out to two of the top experts in the country, relationship expert Dr. Pepper Schwartz and social science researcher Dr. James Witte. I shared my mission with them and asked if they'd help me create an interactive online survey to compare people's relationships around the world. We began compiling questions about the innermost workings of relationships, and we did not hold back. Some examples: *What is your number-one sexual fantasy? What secrets do you keep from your spouse? Have you ever had an affair? What do you most want from your partner that you're not getting?* Before we knew it we had 1,300 questions! I just knew the answers could help not only my relationship but also those of my less than happy friends and many others.

Ultimately, we wanted to learn what was normal for the happiest couples, and contrast their norms with those of less happy partners. Our plan was to collect a massive amount of data, which we then would sort and compare across groups by age, gender, duration of relationship, ethnicity, income, religion, family size, and nationality. This would tell us how factors such as economics, cultural influences, or having kids can affect a couple's relationship.

Fortunately, Dr. Schwartz and Dr. Witte were just as curious as I was and saw the potential in the lessons to be found in those comparisons of positive and negative norms. But how to get that mass of data? *Reader's Digest*, with 70 million global readers, agreed to be our first media partner. In a matter of months Dr. Witte's team had collected information, including many personal anecdotes, from over 25,000 respondents. Using an unprecedented survey technology, Dr. Witte began to analyze the results.

Throughout this process, we picked up an array of tools that Mark and I began to apply to our own relationship. These techniques and practices turned out to be surprisingly simple—and *very* effective! By learning from the data and making simple changes to the choices, interactions, and activities we considered normal, we were able to reinvent—and, more important, reignite—our marriage. We found ourselves more in love and happier than ever. Our new normal reflected the marriage we'd both been missing, one we both needed to be happy, healthy, and fulfilled together. With this proof of process, our team knew we could help other couples, too.

Although our project had barely gotten lift-off at this point, Dr. Schwartz, Dr. Witte, and I envisioned the resulting book, *The Normal Bar*, as a unique relationship resource. We would reveal in detail how people lived their lives together and how each partner's choices affected the success of their sex lives; whether or not they felt loved and appreciated enough; how they felt about themselves; whether they felt fairly or respectfully treated in the relationships. We'd look at styles of communication and intimacy and styles of personal care, housekeeping, and philosophies about finance. In other words, we'd peel back the veneer of couple life and look deep inside to find out what people actually do in every important aspect of their relationships. Our readers would gain a vast array of insights and tools— not because we thought anyone should become more "normal" in the average sense, but so that they could see the scope of possibilities and create their own unique version of a more fulfilling "normal."

The Internet offered us the means to give our survey the scope we envisioned without sacrificing scientific relevance. Back in the 1970s Shere Hite sent out 100,000 questionnaires, but had to base her famous *Hite Report on Female Sexuality* on only a 4% response. Masters and Johnson based their classics, *Human Sexual Response* and *Human Sexual Inadequacy*, on the intimate behavior of 510 couples. By contrast, thanks to today's online technology, we had the ability to go global, reaching tens of thousands of individuals and drilling down much more deeply than previous surveys into our respondents' attitudes, practices, and beliefs.

We enlisted AOL, the Huffington Post, and AARP as additional media partners. We had our survey translated into multiple languages. By the time Dr. Witte began crunching all the information on which this book is based, we had extensive groundbreaking data from more than 70,000 individuals around the world and 1.7 million data points. And the survey is still going strong!

We know this book is going to change lives—even *your* life!—in a very good way. I know because it's changed my husband's and mine. Happiness is a gift every couple deserves. So read on, and enjoy *your* new normal.

CHRISANNA NORTHRUP,
creator and coauthor of *The Normal Bar*

CHAPTER 1

The Normal Bar Is . . .

"I normally use the key."
"Well, I strive to be different."

Are you normal in the way you conduct your relationship?

If you're like most of the people we asked, the answer is no—or at least you hope you're not. "Being normal is boring, and I'm not boring," was the sentiment we heard most often. Many people, in fact, told us they'd do almost anything to *avoid* being "normal."

But suppose we asked, "In your interaction with your significant other, are you extremely happy and sexually satisfied the majority of the time?" If normal means being happy and sexually satisfied, you'd probably *like* to be able to answer yes. So the next question is, how can you attain—and sustain—this kind of normal? Or, put another way, what are the real life keys to a happy relationship?

These questions lie at the heart of *The Normal Bar*. We set out to ask people around the world, first, *what* are the most common attitudes and practices in relationships, or what constitutes the "bar" of normalcy; second, *how* do the "normal bars" of satisfied and dissatisfied couples typically differ; and, finally, what can we learn from these different understandings of normal to help people *change* their relationships for the better?

> The Normal Bar *provides you with a compass and a toolbox so that you can get as close to or as far away from normal as you see fit.*

As you'll see from our findings, what people are *assumed* to be doing in private often bears little or no resemblance to what they actually do. Cultural stereotypes and the media's fantasies of romance and lust have little to do with what really goes on in relationships, especially since conduct varies over time and across geographic boundaries. Our goal, then, was to drill deep, through and beyond common assumptions, to find out just how typical different romantic and domestic habits truly are—and how different interpretations of behavior correlate with personal and relationship happiness. For instance:

- Does the average couple kiss once a day, once a week, once a month, or even less—and how does the frequency of kissing line up with their satisfaction in the relationship?

- Is everyone having a *lot* of sex—or is that level of intimacy pretty rare for everyone except newlyweds?
- Does money still predict who makes the rules in a relationship, or have things changed radically as women have become an increasingly important part of the workforce?
- How often do we lie to our partners; and is honesty really the best way to keep peace in the household?

We created an unprecedented interactive relationship survey (see our Appendix for details about the precise methodology) that asked each participant hundreds of questions about the inner workings of compatibility, romance, affection, communication, sex, money, daily decision making, and emotional connection. Then, by linking the survey through Web sites with millions of viewers—such sites as AARP, Huffington Post, *Reader's Digest,* and AOL—we collected data from more than 70,000 men and women around the world (in countries including Canada, England, France, Italy, Spain, Hungary, Australia, New Zealand, the Philippines, and China). Finally, as the data streamed in, we mapped behavior globally and tracked the patterns and averages, so that readers could pinpoint exactly where they lined up on the Normal Bar of personal and relationship happiness.

Think of the Normal Bar as a tool you can use to compare different areas of your relationship with typical behavior among others in your age, gender, or cultural group. (We'll break these group norms down for you, and you may be surprised to see how they differ.) Each of the chapters to come will examine aspects of couples' lives that affect their happiness and overall satisfaction, from their first weeks and months together, through the day-to-day strains of living together, to the challenges that may threaten their staying together long term. If you find that your own normal in a particular area isn't working for your relationship, look to the Normal Bar to see what typically works best for others.

To maximize the usefulness of this information, in each chapter we'll also suggest simple tools or exercises that can help you and your partner reduce conflict, resentment, and stress. "Normal" habits often outlive their usefulness, but the good news is that most couples can, if they choose, rejuvenate their love at any age by creating a new normal. *The Normal Bar* offers the practical advice you'll need to make this shift.

Don't worry: We're not saying that you have to be "normal" to have a thriving love life, but we will show you which behaviors tend to make for the happiest and strongest couples. You can then use this information to reassess and refine your relationship to your own specifications. Our goal is simply to give you a compass and a toolbox to help move your personal normal into the zone your heart desires.

How Does the Normal Bar Work?

"If I don't do everything, nothing gets done." —female, 38, separated after a 12-year marriage

Let's look at a simplified real-life example of how the Normal Bar process works. Behold Bob and Andrea, the full-time working parents of twelve-year-old Jack. Every day for the last thirteen years, Andrea has done all the family laundry. She thought that was normal, so her position on the Normal Bar for laundry is clear: she bears 100% of her family's laundry duty. Bob and Jack, on the other hand, are sitting pretty at 0% of that responsibility.

Over the years, however, Andrea has become resentful of this norm. She doesn't complain or say anything about it, but she's started

"Honey, are you trying to tell me something?"

to snap at Jack and Bob whenever they ask for clean socks. The guys, meanwhile, have no idea what's gotten into Andrea. It seems like such a minor issue. They dismiss her growing agitation, but that only increases Andrea's resentment. When Bob can't find his boxers, she lays into him for even asking where they are. The emotional climate in the house is getting worse, but to Andrea, Bob, and Jack it's a mystery why. They all *assume* it's normal for the wife and mother to do all the laundry, so this can't possibly be the real problem—or can it?

Desperate, Andrea takes a poll of her girlfriends, asking if they do all the laundry in their households. She learns that, while a majority of the wives do all the laundry, there are actually a handful of husbands who do it, and some husbands and wives split the chore—in a few cases, the older kids in the house even help. Most important, from just this small sampling, Andrea learns that a lot of the couples

Andrea 100%

Bob and Kid 0%

Andrea, Bob, and Kid 33%

who share the chore seem to have happier relationships than those in which the wife bears the whole burden 100% of the time. Not only is a different normal possible, but it looks like a different normal might be a *better* normal all around! Armed with this insight, Andrea sees a new way forward.

She gathers her courage and tells her husband and son what she's learned from her friends and how she feels about doing the laundry. To her surprise, Bob and Jack are relieved that the problem isn't something more serious. Bob was starting to think that Andrea was unhappy with him or the relationship, not ever imagining that she was just sick of doing the laundry every day. The solution? Bob and Jack agree to share the responsibility, and Andrea's new normal becomes just a third of her previous duty. This is a norm she can happily accept on an ongoing basis.

Opening the Normal Bar Tool Kit

The smallest issue can erode or even destroy a relationship if it becomes a norm that one of the partners resents. Realizing that a different normal is possible is a vital first step toward addressing the issue and having a clear alternative in mind always makes the process of change less intimidating. But it's not always easy to make the leap from a long-established norm to a preferable one. Old habits sometimes die hard, and your partner might not be as willing to change as you are. That's why we offer true stories, advice, and tools in every chapter in this book to help you and your partner get to your new normal.

These suggestions are culled from the tactics and exercises our respondents have used most effectively to improve overall satisfaction and sexual connection in their relationships. After analyzing our data and hearing how our happiest couples solved problems, we were astounded by the simplicity of many of these practices and the ease with which they can be woven into daily life. Even a small adjustment can make a big change and can turn a pattern of habits that couples don't like into one that supports them and their relationships. Some of the tools might seem obvious to you when you read about them, but what's not obvious is the critical difference they can make to a relationship when actually *used*. For instance, knowing that your partner likes to be told "I love you" is one thing; actually *saying* "I love you" is quite another. Seemingly minor changes can make the difference between living happily ever after together, breaking up, or, worse, staying together and never feeling completely fulfilled.

Think of personal hygiene as an analogy. We've all been told that people who floss their teeth are less likely than non-flossers to have plaque buildup and cavities. But let's pretend that we've surveyed thousands of people and learned that those who don't floss *every day* have a 75% greater chance of having their teeth fall out. Maybe because you knew flossing was good for your teeth you normally flossed from time to time, but after hearing this startling data, wouldn't you consider making *daily* flossing part of your normal routine? Minor adjustments in your "relationship hygiene" can also make a big difference in your health as a couple.

Emphasizing the importance of certain behaviors by presenting new and convincing data about those behaviors is the heart and soul of this book. We'll share the insights and experiences of people all over the world. And while the advice and strategies for constructing a new normal may appear simple, never doubt their potential to help you achieve real change.

Let's get started!

PART

I

Getting Together

CHAPTER 2

Are You the One for Me?

The instant I saw her I knew we were meant for each other. It was love at first sight.

Doesn't that sound romantic? Such electric moments are a staple of love stories, and many of us grow up believing they're the truest sign of "true" love. So we wanted to know: Do these moments actually occur in real life?

Yes! At least they did for 28% of women and 48% of men in our survey. The sharp difference between the sexes might surprise you, but it's actually in line with other research that shows men are more romantic than women, more likely to fall in love because of the way a potential partner looks, and more likely to feel love when there is extreme sexual attraction. Women tend to be more wary, and most need to know more about a partner's character and background before they'll allow the deeper emotions to develop.

But what about the premium we place on love at first sight? Does this immediate charge correlate to happier long-term relationships? Not in overall contentment, according to the Normal Bar. Those who have eased into love gradually are just as likely to be happy together as those who were hit by a lightning bolt of passion on day one.

Enduring Passion

Couples who fell in love at first sight are more likely to still *be sexually satisfied with each other in midlife.*

There is, however, one critical area where that initial lightning bolt seems to leave an enduring impact: People who fell in love at first sight are more likely than gradual lovers to claim satisfaction with their present *sex* life—even after decades together! In fact, the group most likely to report this sexual boon was middle-aged men and women between the ages of 45 and 54. This *might* indicate that intense attraction early on in the rela-

tionship was especially important for the last group of baby boomers. More likely, it means that love at first sight is a strong gauge of sexual interest that will stand the test of time.

Are You with Your Soul Mate?

Love, of course, involves more than attraction—more even than sexual satisfaction. Compatibility is a crucial element as well. Many of us grew up absorbing the message—from fairy tales, Disney movies, romance novels, and perhaps our families—that "true" love depends on finding the one "true" mate who is meant for us: our "soul mate." But what does this mean?

The term *soul mate* has become a popular concept relatively recently and is now widespread—and aspirational. We found that most people think of soul mates as two people who are "right for" each other and belong together. But beyond this sense of belonging, there are some important conceptual variations.

Those who are religious might add more spiritual—and permanent—criteria. "Till death do us part," after all, is standard language in marriage vows exchanged in most churches. We compared people by religion and found that people of all faiths believe

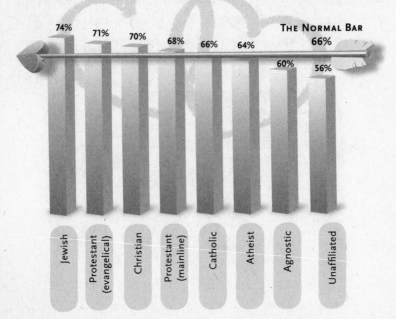

Believe Their Current Partners Are Their Soul Mates

74% Jewish
71% Protestant (evangelical)
70% Christian
68% Protestant (mainline)
66% Catholic
64% Atheist
60% Agnostic
56% Unaffiliated

THE NORMAL BAR 66%

in this concept. Furthermore, most religious people believe that they have found and are with their own soul mates!

Curiously, the percentage of soul mates drops significantly among nonbelievers and those not affiliated with a particular religion. Or perhaps they're just less inclined to identify their partners by that term. But while the religious divide is intriguing, the much more important news is that more than half of *all* people we asked said their current partners *are* their soul mates. Some believe in the one true soul mate concept, while others believe there could be several "true" mates for each person. Either way, a solid majority believe they're with the person they're meant to love.

So . . . are the people who believe they're with their soul mate more satisfied with their sex lives? Yes! Among the soul mated, 82% of men and 83% of women said they're *very* satisfied with their sex lives. Of course, first-rate sex could be one of the criteria for identifying your partner as a soul mate in the first place, but general happiness plays an important role as well. If having a soul mate means that your sexual and emotional lives are well in sync, then

"We are so connected . . ."

our findings suggest that there are a lot of very contented couples in the world.

We Are So Connected . . .

We've all seen couples who appear to be obvious soul mates—who finish each other's sentences, look at each other lovingly, and just seem to be perfectly matched. Then there are those other couples, who always seem to be bickering, talking over each other, gesturing angrily or accusingly, couples we assume to be miserable only to find out this is just how they relate, and somehow it works for them. The truth is, none of us can judge another couple's happiness or know, from the outside, whether they should be together. So we decided to ask couples to tell us from their own perspectives what connects them.

BEWARE

After six years together as a couple, 20% fewer men and women still find their partners as attractive as they did in year one.

Here are some of the top physical and emotional indicators that make a difference in the overall sense of connection within relationships.

Are you physically attracted to your partner?

It's nice to see that most (74%) of the general population are *extremely* attracted to their partners. Less happily, 22% of partners told us they are less attracted than they "used to be," and 4% are totally disenchanted. The longer a relationship has lasted, it seems, the more likely it is that the sexual spark will have dimmed. Among respondents in the first year of a relationship, 92% told us they find their partners extremely attractive. Among those in their sixth to ninth year of a relationship, just 68% still reported that level of appeal. Coincidentally, the Normal Bar shows that there also happens to be a big drop in couples' efforts to stay fit and attractive for each other between years six and nine. After the ninth year, however, the decline slows, so that at twenty-one years plus, 58% said they still find their partners extremely attractive.

But here's the unexpected kicker. Among couples who told us they are *unhappy* with their relationships, 57% still find their partners extremely appealing! Even among those who *hate* their sex lives, 55% of both men and women still are attracted to their partners. While looks are part of the package, they clearly don't matter enough to save a relationship that's not working in other departments. This is equally true for both men and women.

On the other hand, we found a surprising number of people for whom looks don't matter at all. One-fifth of all people who are extremely happy in their relationships told us they've lost their attraction for their mates and still are extremely happy with the relationship. This represents a sizable minority for whom physical appearance has receded into the background. With age, it's normal for some people to lose interest in the sexual or physical appeal of their partners, while other factors, such as companionship, intellectual stimulation, a sense of humor, and emotional comfort come more strongly into play. This is a bit tricky, however, because for attractiveness and sexual desire to become irrelevant, both partners have to feel the same way.

Does similarity or difference create compatibility?

There are two schools of thought here. One says that the more you have in common with your partner, the better your relationship will be. The other says that the less you have in common, the more fascinating you'll be to each other. Which is right? A lot of research on this topic leans toward similarity working best, but according to the Normal Bar the truth lies somewhere in the middle.

Couples who have nothing in common tend to run separate lives and have few shared—or satisfying—bonds. But couples who have everything in common are less likely to introduce one another to new things—unless they explore new endeavors together. Let's see how similarities and differences specifically impact couple happiness.

INTERNATIONAL CHECKPOINT	
People who are extremely attracted to their partner:	
Spain	80%
Philippines	79%
China	75%
United States	74%
France	72%
Canada	71%
England	71%
Italy	67%

Are you and your partner similar or different?

We began by asking people if they considered themselves to be more similar to or different from their partners. More than half said they are more different in nature. When we measured the happiness of these contrary couples, the majority (75%) fell into the slightly unhappy group. What about the 45% who said they are more similar to their partner? A whopping 95% described their relationships as extremely happy. They felt being similar to their partners helped strengthen their relationships.

The Normal Bar, then, suggests that people with different personalities and few shared interests may have more difficulty relating to each other as a couple than those who are very similar to one another. That's not to say that you are setting yourself up for disaster if you and your partner are very different. However, you will have to acknowledge and respect those differences and make an effort to find areas of common cause, pleasure, and agreement. Some differences *are* interesting, but it can become alienating if you have nothing in common.

Does sharing the same religious beliefs make a difference?

Religion is often raised as a major consideration when choosing a mate, so we wanted to know if couples who differ in their faith or beliefs experience more friction in their relationships. An overwhelming 80% said no, it doesn't hurt the relationship. Couples can have separate religious preferences and it seems to have no impact on their overall happiness. Most partners expressed support for each other's choices.

One caveat, though: We did not identify respondents with fundamentalist beliefs. Most fundamentalists belong to churches and communities that shape a great part of their social and family lives, as well as their religious lives. Thus religious differences would likely pose a larger challenge to a couple in which one partner is fundamentalist and the other is not.

Does sharing the same social or political views make or break a relationship?

When two people have different views on social or political issues it can definitely make for interesting conversation, but what about living with someone whose political views are vastly different? Our first surprise when we probed this question was the discovery that only a third of all our respondents *do* share the same social or political views as their partners! How are the other 67% managing?

Better than you might imagine. Among these politically mismatched partners, 59% said their contrasting views cause no problem in the relationship. Only 9% said those differences do cause big strains in the household. Clearly it's possible for couples to get along even if they have opposing ideas about how the larger world should be run.

Perhaps it all depends on how important those views are to each person or how intensely or respectfully they discuss their views.

People who share different political views have to be, dare we say, *politic* when they talk to one another. Some people learn how to diplomatically agree or disagree. Others manage to listen respectfully and steer clear of certain hot-button topics. One couple told us they belong to two different parties, fund different candidates, and feel very differently about such incendiary topics as abortion, gun control, immigration, and public health. Yet they kid each other affectionately about each other's "way out" views and manage to keep their political activities very separate from the rest of their life, which is otherwise highly intertwined. Not everyone can or wants to maintain a norm like this, but this couple has been successful at it for forty years.

POLITICS AND PASSION

Two-thirds of couples do not agree with each other's politics.

Fewer than 10% of these couples say this seriously strains their relationships.

What I'm not getting from my partner . . .

"I love her to death, but I could always use a bit of alone time. I enjoy wandering around on my own, away from people. I can't do that nearly as much as I used to." —male, 25, never married, in a 5-year relationship, no kids

"I feel happy to be in a relationship with a very kind man who I trust and respect, but there is no physical intimacy, and that is difficult for me to accept." —female, 42, in a 12-year relationship, no kids

"Lack of communication, lack of shared interest, lack of shared goals or worldview, disappointing physical relationship." —female, 29, married 6 years, no kids

"My boyfriend lets me be myself and do my own independent thing. But I wish he was more adventurous and independent and had more friends." —female, 34, in a 9-year relationship, no kids

MEN WANT MORE

Is sex *the #1 thing that men want more of?*

No, communication *is.*

"It is as if we're beyond the expiration date. We are in a sexless marriage, highly stressed, and have children with special needs. The economy doesn't help." —male, 46, married 17 years, with kids

"Would be extremely happy if he wasn't married to someone else." —female, 54, divorced, no kids

"My wife is an excellent partner, but the romantic spark seems to be missing. Or I am just messed up. Not sure which." —male, 38, married 14 years, with kids

When we asked guys in unhappy relationships to tell us what they want most from their partners that they're not getting, we expected sex to top the list. After all, the media would have us believe that all men just love sex and can't get enough of it. But when we posed this question, we offered nine answers to choose from, and sex was *not* their number-one wish. No, the winner was communication! According to 28% of these unhappy guys, their partners just don't talk or listen to them attentively enough. Affection came in second, and sex was down in third place.

The complaints weren't all that different among unhappy women. Communication also ranked at the top of the list for 40% of them. And women also hankered for affection in second place. But while sex ranked third for men, women's third wish was for financial stability.

Just for fun, we decided to see how these findings among unhappy partners compared to the wishes of those who are extremely happy in their relationships. The winning answer, among 36% of contented women and 40% of satisfied men was: *nothing!* These lucky people are getting all their needs met. In second place? A virtual tie between sex for men, at 25%, and communication for 24% of women.

All told, these results indicate that communication is a big deal, whether we're in a happy relationship or not. And this is true worldwide. Respondents in almost every country we queried said that communication was their biggest relationship issue.

Only the French disagreed. In France, the most common missing ingredient is affection, with communication in second place. This stymied us because, when it came to romance, France had all other countries beat. French men and women reported the most romantic gestures— gifts, getaways, etc. Yet 22% of French men and women said their partner's affection is what they miss most in their relationships. A reminder that there's much more to love than romance.

⊕ INTERNATIONAL
CHECKPOINT

What men and women in France say is the number-one thing they're missing from their partner: *affection*.

What Kind of Partner Is Your Partner?

To find out what kind of partnerships make for the most loving relationships, we asked individuals to categorize their partners as a passionate lover, best friend, good friend, teammate, sparring partner, or sworn enemy. To simplify things, we made sure they could pick only one category.

Sworn enemies and sparring partners

Men and women who view their partners as a sworn enemy or a sparring partner also expressed dissatisfaction in their overall relationship. No surprise there.

What *is* interesting is that this level of animosity is about the same in all the countries that participated in the study. Happily only a small percentage of people worldwide see their partners in such adversarial terms.

INTERNATIONAL CHECKPOINT

Couples who are sworn enemies and sparring partners:

United States	8%
Hungary	8%
Canada	6%
England	5%
Spain	5%

Good friends or best friends

Do friends make good life partners and lovers? Yes, but only as long as they consider each other a *best* friend. Among couples who are "best friends," 36% described their relationships as very happy or better; but only 16% of couples who are "good friends" felt that way about themselves. More "best friends" even than "passionate lovers" said they are very happy or extremely happy in their relationships.

And how does the "best friend" stack up in bed? Among those who regard their

INTERNATIONAL CHECKPOINT

Couples who are all-around *best* friends:

England	47%
United States	36%
Australia	36%
China	35%
Latin America	35%

partners as best friends, 29% of men and 35% of women said they
have a very satisfying sex life. But the norm drops precipitously for
those who are in the "good friend" category; only 8% of those men
and women are sexually satisfied. Beware if you ever hear your partner
refer to you as a "good friend"!

Passionate lover

In America just 26% of respondents described their partners as a
"passionate lover." Other countries turn up the heat, and France and
Italy live up to their reputations on this one!

Partners of "passionate lovers" are predictably the most satisfied with sex, but even
great sex isn't enough to guarantee overall
happiness. One-third of extremely happy
men and women said that their partners are
passionate lovers, compared to 40% of men
and 44% of women who also said they are
extremely happy and with their best friends.
Perhaps it's comforting to know that a rela-
tionship can be happy even if a man or woman doesn't see a partner
as passionate.

INTERNATIONAL CHECKPOINT

Couples who are
passionate lovers:

Italy	62%
France	55%
Philippines	46%
Spain	44%
Latin America	33%
Canada	30%

Teammate

We expected people who picked "teammate" as their category to feel very close to
their partners. We were wrong! It turns out
that most people globally do not consider
"teammate" to be a term of endearment.
Those who chose to put their partners
in this category actually were most likely
to describe their relationships as slightly

INTERNATIONAL CHECKPOINT

Is your lover your
teammate?

Australia/ New Zealand	19%
Scandinavia	16%
Africa	15%
Canada	13%
United States	13%

unhappy, perhaps more of a shared obligation than a love affair. Parents were no more likely than childless people to categorize their partners as teammates, so the size of the domestic "team" was not a deciding issue. The correlation unfortunately was with dissatisfaction.

New Normal Advice

Relationships follow a natural progression that cannot be avoided. Over the years we learn and grow, maybe have kids, focus on our careers, and find time for things we enjoy. It's inevitable that the relationship will evolve and change course. The Normal Bar shows us that most happy couples start out with a passionate connection, but eventually come to cherish each other as best friends. But what happens when you and your partner fall into the teammate category or, worse, become sworn enemies? Can you also *correct* course?

Consider Rhonda and Dwayne. Their relationship began with the thrill of falling in love at first sight. While hiking with separate groups of friends one day, they passed each other on the hiking trail and the connection between them was instantaneous and electric. With compatible interests and ages and a strong mutual physical attraction, they were off to a great start. They dated for two years, then married and shifted from being passionate lovers to best friends. They started having kids while focusing on their careers and saving money to buy a home. Gradually, the best friendship downgraded to good friendship. Then they were more like teammates in survival mode. Their relationship had become efficient but not passionate, organized but not intimate.

While this is a very common scenario, having kids or pursuing a career doesn't mean you have to slip into the teammate category. Putting time aside for each other, going out on date nights, and making sure to continue to do the things you enjoy together are crucial at this stage. Unfortunately, Rhonda and Dwayne, like many couples, didn't know how important this kind of relationship maintenance is and by the time they realized their marriage was in jeopardy, family and work demands made romance and intimate conversation almost impossible. Their norm had slipped from extremely happy to good, with unhappy on the horizon.

The teammate bond became more and more prominent, and they found themselves bickering whenever family, household, or work issues arose. Most of their conversations became arguments about who was doing what around the house or with the kids and who ought to be pulling more weight. Pretty soon Dwayne was going out of his way to avoid spending time alone with his wife. Hurt by the growing distance between them, Rhonda stopped trying to break down communication barriers and just kept busy with her job and the kids. She didn't look forward to making love anymore, partly because she was tired, but mainly because she was angry. They both knew they were growing apart but neither of them knew how to stop.

What could you do in Dwayne and Rhonda's place? First, think about what you want in a best friend. The one person you can always go to no matter what. The one you truly enjoy spending time with because it's fun and you have a lot in common. The one with whom you share all your good days and all your bad days. The one with whom you feel comfortable saying anything—because you can trust you won't be criticized or attacked in response. Perhaps the three most important elements of best friendship are communication, trust, and quality time. Best friends take equal responsibility for protecting the friendship and mutually make sure to reserve attention for one another.

If you're giving your time to others instead of your partner, you'll lose your partner as a best friend. To repair this situation it's essential to recognize where your relationship is on the compatibility bar and make the decision to change it. Changing your relationship from teammates to best friends or best friends to passionate lovers is a relatively easy transition to make. The change from sworn enemies to best friends is also doable, but it might take the insights of a therapist or more major commitment to communication and quality time.

To change their compatibility norm, Rhonda and Dwayne each needed to take responsibility for keeping the other up to date and involved in the most important aspects of their daily life. They didn't need to call a dramatic summit meeting; they simply had to make it a priority to spend more time connecting. Vital changes were as easy as suggesting they do something they both enjoy together, or something that one partner knows the other enjoys. They could also take turns choosing something new to try together. Dwayne loved tennis and hadn't played in years; Rhonda liked tennis somewhat, but wasn't that great at it. So Rhonda invited Dwayne to play tennis and asked him to give her some lessons. This helped them reconnect as if they were best friends.

What could be simpler? Treat your partner like your best friend, and chances are that you'll soon find you *are* best friends. Reconnect by having fun together, and talk to your partner about your day rather than confiding first in others. If this sounds easy, that's because it is! It's small changes like this that have proven to create happier relationships.

Tool 1 ▶ Just You and Me

A lot of busy couples share most of their activities with friends or family. That's fine up to a point, but every couple also needs experiences that they alone share. Meet right after work and go to a movie together, making time to trade your thoughts about the film over dinner afterward. Or reconnect with your partner by signing up for a class or arranging an outing that you both will enjoy—a hike, yoga, painting, golf. If you're not sure what new activities your partner would enjoy, ask!

TOOL 2 ▶ How Well Do I Know You? Game

There used to be a quiz show called *The Newlywed Game* on American television, in which the host would ask new husbands and wives—separately—about their own and each other's habits. The newlywed couples that could best predict each other's answers won the game.

How well would you do if you played that game? Just for fun, play it every so often with each other. Here are a few questions to get you started: *Who do you think is my best friend? If I could pick anyone famous to have over to dinner, who would it be? What is something that I've always wanted to try?*

No judgments if you or your partner answers incorrectly. This is just an entertaining way to learn more about each other—because there's *always* more to learn. That's one of the reasons relationships stay interesting and survive!

TOOL 3 ▶ It Takes Two to Tango

You can take this literally or figuratively—either way, it works! Dancing is a wonderful way to turn a teammate into a lover and best friend. Dancing together, especially if you learn a sexy and intricate step like the tango, turns up the heat, turns on the endorphins (those hormones that make you feel happy), and helps you enjoy being in each other's arms. You'll explore a new way of being together.

If the tango is not for you (it requires coordination and a lot of dramatic flare), you could learn line dancing, ballroom, swing, or even pairs ice skating or roller skating. Even if it's just an occasional activity, collaborating to music and holding each other is good for pushing a partnership into a new, more intense, intimate, and happy category.

TOOL 4 ▶ Form a Book Club of Two

What books do you both enjoy? Poetry? Classic novels? Short stories? True crime? Make it a couple activity to read and discuss them. Read out loud to each other. Discuss and laugh about the characters and stories. You could hold your book club on Saturday mornings or for a short time on certain weeknights. Let your reading open up new and interesting dimensions of your own story as a couple.

CHAPTER 3

A Little Romance . . . Or a Lot

"Frank boycotts Valentine's Day . . . says it's a big marketing scheme."

"How's that working for him?"

Romantic comedies have always been popular. Romance novels sell by the millions. Everybody loves a good romance, and almost everybody craves romantic love.

Or do they?

This was one of the first questions we wanted to explore in our survey. But before we could ask about people's romantic norms, we had to define what we meant by "romance."

"I'm not sure anymore what is implied by 'romantic.' Is that a man holding the door? Paying for dinner? Planning the date? Flowers? I find men aren't romantic anymore." —female, 24, divorced

It's not actually all that complicated. Loving gestures produce pleasure and deep feelings of excitement, love, and connection. The connection feels intense—special and intrinsically magical. And there's an element of surprise. The sweetest part is the discovery of your beloved's desire to thrill and please you. That's the essence of romance.

It's not just about celebrating Valentine's Day, planning a date, buying flowers, or paying for dinner. In fact, the idea of romance is often diminished and narrowed by such "romantic" conventions, which can lead the person buying the flowers or planning the date to think that's all it takes to create romance. The gestures then can seem empty or manipulative, resulting in disappointment and even alienation. Real romance *can* be expressed by a special gift or event, but only if the offerings reflect genuine and mutual love.

Isn't It Romantic?

Romance is the pleasurable feeling of excitement and mystery associated with love.

How Important Is Romance?

In the beginning of a relationship, just seeing each other is a romantic turn-on. Both men and women dress up to please their new partners and strive to surprise and delight them. Those first vulnerable moments when love is declared—and reciprocated—represent the height of romance. They also build an important foundation for the vows and promises that lie ahead. As a relationship deepens, romantic behavior becomes more subtle, expressed through actions rather than words. Simply holding hands, research shows, plays a powerful role in securing love. Some couples dance together, others hike or spend Saturday mornings in bed.

Early romantic moments help love grow, but they need to continue as the relationship develops. Otherwise the romantic expectations that were established in the beginning will be dashed, and this can lead to real unhappiness. Couples who stop spending romantic time together often lose sexual interest in each other. We call this romantic deprivation.

INTERNATIONAL CHECKPOINT

Who wants *more* romance?

	MEN	WOMEN
United States	64%	63%
China	47%	69%
France	43%	54%
Philippines	42%	63%
Italy	42%	53%
Spain	37%	53%

Romance—Who says they need more of it?

When we asked people around the globe who wanted more romance, we found that almost equal numbers of American men and women feel deprived, but in the rest of the world far more women than men lust after romance. Only about a third of women in the Philippines and China feel sufficiently romanced, and in France, Italy, and Spain, not quite half are satisfied. Men in most countries fare slightly better. Italy, Spain, France, and the Philippines have the largest percentages of satisfied men, but only in Spain does the number of well-romanced men top 60%.

We weren't surprised to learn that women generally would like more romance in their lives, but we uncovered a big surprise when we dug deeper into romantic attitudes among couples. Although more women than men globally feel deprived of romance, more than a third more *men* than women around the world said it bothered them "a lot" that their significant other wasn't more romantic. Apparently men suffer more than women when they perceive a romance deficit.

Bothers Them "A Lot" That Their Partner Is Not More Romantic

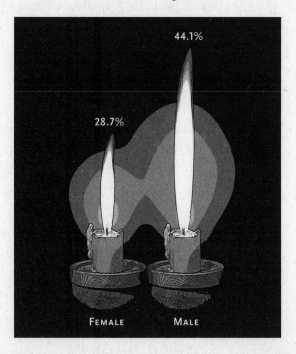

44.1%

28.7%

FEMALE   MALE

Romantic desires

Fortunately, our data tell us that men and women have pretty similar expectations when it comes to the particulars of romantic behavior. Asked to describe their ideal romantic evening, most women said they like to get dressed up and have dinner at a fine restaurant, drink a special bottle of wine, and then make love either at home or at an upscale hotel (a location favored by women with kids). Most men said the same thing, just a little differently. They'll dress up to please their partners, take them out to dinner at a favorite location, then go somewhere private and exchange full-body massages or take a bath together—and have sex all night.

Both these "normal" versions of a romantic evening include attempts to make the night special, with some privacy, excitement, lovemaking, and feelings of deep connectedness. Throw in a few elements of surprise or luxury and you have an ideal romantic date. Here are some other ideas that hit these same benchmarks:

"Going on a picnic to our favorite secluded park; talking, making out, and pleasuring each other for hours in the shade." —female, 24, dating seriously

"Going somewhere very discreet, like by the lake, have some drinks and

GLOBAL ROMANCE

The universal ideal of a romantic date varies internationally only in its setting. Non-American couples prefer more outdoor locales, such as beaches, ocean landscapes, and snowy mountaintops. Historical buildings and castles are also popular venues.

talk to each other and maybe go skinny-dipping!" —female, 35, married, no kids

"Steak dinner, come home and cuddle in front of the fire with a glass of wine." —female, 45, married, with kids

"We would love to be in Europe walking hand in hand, touring and sharing a glass of wine while we people-watch, then go back to our B&B and finish the day off by making love and falling asleep in his arms." —female, 50, married, with kids

"A fairy-tale romantic evening where it would feel like we are the only two people around." —female, 35, same-sex domestic partnership

"Afternoon movie, dinner out somewhere she is excited to try, then TV at home while we make out before heading to the bedroom." —male, 38, committed relationship

"Take her anywhere she wants to go, then great sex after." —male, 55, married, with kids

"Dinner and a long conversation. Her wanting to make love to me without checking her Facebook." —male, 48, married, with kids

"She would arrange for child care without my having to do it. Figure out a way to pay for a night out without it coming back on me. Listening to calm/friendly live music. Asking about things I'm interested in. Not falling asleep early or complaining." —male, 49, married, with kids

"Un refuge de montagne, en dehors il neige, et moi et lui seul. Un dîner en face de la cheminée avec un bon vin et la bonne nourriture, promenades sur la neige et de rester nus toute la journée dans un chalet." (English translation: *"We're in a mountain cottage, it's snowing outside, and he and I all alone. A dinner in front of the fireplace with good wine and good food, walks in the snow, and staying naked all day in the chalet."*)—female living in France, 33, married, with kids

Most romantic memory

We also asked people to tell us their most romantic memory from their current relationship. Most involved unexpected gestures, but significantly, only a few mentioned extravagant trips or gifts. A large number of women talked about passionate kisses and love notes left for them in surprising places. Here are some other standout memories from women:

"We had just arrived at a motel while on a road trip vacation. We checked into the motel, but before we got to the room he started kissing me passionately in a kind of secluded area. I still think about that kiss often."—female, 55, married, with kids

"When he replaced the little flags sticking out of some Hershey kisses with his own flags with things he loves about me on them."—female, 28, married, no kids

"When I returned from a trip out of state, she hung Christmas lights (which I love) throughout the room for ambience and then ran a bubble bath for me to enjoy."—female, 37, same-sex domestic partnership

"He put me on his Harley, rode me down to the boat ramp, and gave me the sweetest, most sensuous kiss I've ever experienced in my life. My knees melted."—female, 35, married, with kids

"After one of our dates, he walked me up to my front door, and it was raining. I asked him to kiss me on the porch because I always wanted to be kissed in the rain like in the movies. He then grabbed my hand and dragged me to the yard and gave me a slow, tender, passionate kiss."—female, 25, serious commitment

Men's favorite romantic memories centered on moments when they felt especially loved, often during sex or while kissing, touching, or talking:

"Unbeknownst to her, I packed clothes, toiletries, jewelry for my wife; arranged for child care; and took her to a beach cottage two hours away from home, all without her knowing about it beforehand. We had a magical full weekend at the beach."—male, 48, married, with kids

"When she wore nothing underneath her dress during Valentine's dinner 10 years ago."—male, 45, married, with kids

"Niagara Falls trip without children after 10 years of marriage. Wicked sex. Great times together out of bed."—male, 45, married, with kids

"Re-created our first date on our anniversary."—male, 35, married, no kids

"Her gently touching me in conversations with others."—male, 55, married, with kids

"Our 12-mile hike along the Na Pali Coast, Kauai, watching the sunset. Later, lying together on the Kalalau Beach, looking up at the stars and making love."—male, 47, married 16 years, with kids

Romance creates desire, and desire often expresses itself romantically. It's a simple and obvious loop, yet so many people ache for more romance and more mutual desire in their lives. What we learned from the thousands of comments we received is that romance naturally blossoms in some people when they want their partners to love them—or to love or want them *more*. It also emerges when one partner is feeling loved and wants to show gratitude in a way that the other will appreciate. Sadly, the loop often frays when one partner makes romantic gestures out of these genuine needs and hopes, and the gestures are unappreciated, unnoticed, or unreciprocated. If this pattern continues, over time the romantic overtures will cease.

Forms of Romantic Expression

The Normal Bar data suggest that romantic expression may be more important in your relationship than you realize. But just how important? How much is enough? And what impact do *specific* romantic acts have on our relationships?

Romantic gifts

Giving your partner a romantic gift for a special holiday, anniversary, or birthday can be as simple as writing or quoting a poem, sending a love note or flowers, or offering a relaxing massage. However, the Normal Bar data show us that giving *nothing* is definitely toxic and, over time, will actually harm your relationship.

When we looked at Americans, we found a strong connection between gift giving and sexual satisfaction. Of those who said they never receive romantic gifts of any kind, 64% of women and 88% of men said they're also dissatisfied with their sex lives. Now, that could simply mean that people who have a broken sexual connection are much less likely to feel or evoke feelings of romance, but gift giving can also play an important role in repairing relationships. It can promote a better connection, especially if that gift reflects genuine love.

It seems that the French and Italians are far ahead of Americans on this message. While less than half of American men and women feel they receive enough romantic presents, two-thirds of French women and three-fourths of Italian women feel they get plenty! And more than three-fourths of both French and Italian men are satisfied with the romantic mementos they receive from their partners. All told, French women seem to be the international stars of gift giving, with their men not far behind.

If you don't give romantic gifts, it's worth considering *why* you don't. Were gifts not given in your family when you were growing up? If so, the habit may seem forced and false. Or maybe you've offered gifts in the past but your partner is so picky that you never seem to give the right thing, and you've just given up trying. Perhaps your partner insists that presents are a needless waste of money, and you

---

🌐 INTERNATIONAL CHECKPOINT

WOMEN who aren't receiving romantic gifts:

United States	52%
France	33%
Italy	25%

MEN who aren't receiving romantic gifts:

United States	62%
Italy	25%
France	23%

agree. Or maybe your partner tells you your relationship is so solid that you don't need to bother with gifts. These are all compelling justifications, but they can mislead you into unintentionally undermining your relationship. This is especially true if your partner is discouraging your gift giving.

Even when your partner says, "It's OK, you don't need to get me a present for my birthday," what he or she really is saying most likely is, "If I have to tell you that I want something for my birthday, don't bother getting it, because I know now you don't care enough to do it on your own." It really is the thought—or the lack of thought—that counts. Romantic gifts need to be genuine surprises. They need to come from the heart, not out of a sense of obligation or duty. No one wants to have to *tell* the other person to give; so if you feel the love, by all means, show the love.

Date night

The Normal Bar screams "Date night!" The vast majority of couples who describe themselves as extremely happy also take care to spend time together alone, away from family and work routines. Even after marriage, in other words, they "date." And those dates boost their intimacy and happiness. Only 12% of our extremely happy couples never have date nights.

American couples date more than their international counterparts. More than half of all of our participating international couples never have a date night.

⊕ INTERNATIONAL
    CHECKPOINT

Couples who say they hardly ever or never go out on a date:

France	55%
England	54%
South Asia	54%
Italy	53%
United States	44%

People over fifty are also less likely to go out on dates. Of couples aged fifty-five and older, 56% said they hardly ever or never have date nights. Uh-oh. This may reflect a habit of staying home that many older couples fall into, but it isn't a good norm for any relationship, no matter how long you've been together.

Another excuse is economic, but romantic outings need not be expensive. A date can consist of a walk along the beach, a visit to a museum, a picnic in the park. It's the time together and the shared experience of doing something out of the ordinary that matters, not the tab.

Frequency also counts. If you go out with your partner once a week or even twice a month, you'll do your relationship a great favor. A few times a year is a good effort, but the Normal Bar shows that it's not enough for most people. Dating has to happen regularly enough to become a norm for you.

Romantic vacations

Romantic getaways are an important and necessary variety of dates that all too few couples make part of their norm. Whether vacations consist of a weekend camping trip, a night in a friend's cabin on the lake, or a week abroad, the extra time together and distance from home can help couples discover new aspects of each other and roll through challenges that just never come up in their daily routine. Vacations also generate new and important memories of adventure and exploration that can deepen a relationship.

NEVER EVER?

Three-fourths of all American couples have never taken a romantic vacation.

We were surprised, then, to find that 72% of our respondents *never* take vacations as a couple. The culprit for a full half of these nonvacationers is kids. Finding a sitter for a full weekend can be difficult and expensive. Some couples don't want to be separated from their children. Others feel guilty about using scarce free time to bond as a couple rather than as a family. These are valid feelings and objections, but there is another reality to consider. Children need parents who have a happy, loving, stable relationship. And to achieve that stability, the parents need romantic time alone together as adults. It can be a game changer!

Back rubs

Looking for another way to up your game? Back and neck rubs, the more the better.

The need to touch and be touched is among the most normal of shared needs among mammals. Lions rub against each other, puppies pile on top of puppies, and all primates groom each other. We aren't so different. Massage both shows love and encourages it. If you and your partner exchange massages and back rubs, you are much more likely to be in the extremely happy category on the Normal Bar!

Among the couples who give the highest possible rating to their relationships, 74% of them rub each other's backs! That's a lot of happy people getting touched on a regular basis. And who's doing the rubbing among these happy couples? Eighty percent of the happiest women and 72% of the happiest men *give* rubdowns! Among extremely happy gay men and lesbians, 100% say they give massages on a regular basis.

Passionate kissing

We all know that a kiss is not just a kiss. A truly passionate kiss is in a league of its own. When we watch one on the big screen we get a vicarious thrill. When we get swept up in a steamy embrace ourselves, the feeling of romance is intense. Fortunately, these ultra-kisses are not at all rare. We found that about 70% of all people in relationships kiss passionately, and there's virtually no difference between men and women. (How *often* couples kiss is another matter, but we'll get to that.)

Not unexpectedly, the couples most likely to kiss passionately are young, newly in love, or both. Still, the percentages are reasonably high in every other age group, too. Even among couples who've been together twenty-five years or more, more than half still kiss passionately.

Does all this kissing really matter? When we take a closer look at the nonkissers, the Normal Bar tells us it matters a lot. Of those who said their normal never includes passionate kissing, 76% also said that they are *very dissatisfied* with their sex lives.

It's all connected—the romance, the dates, the kisses, the sex, and the love.

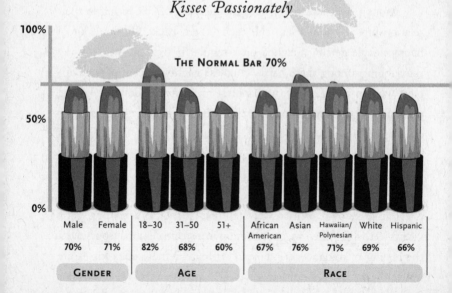

Kisses Passionately

THE NORMAL BAR 70%

	GENDER		AGE			RACE				
	Male	Female	18–30	31–50	51+	African American	Asian	Hawaiian/ Polynesian	White	Hispanic
	70%	71%	82%	68%	60%	67%	76%	71%	69%	66%

New Normal Advice

When she heard the Normal Bar findings about passionate kissing, Sage, a forty-two-year-old mother of three who's been married for sixteen years, asked her husband, Kazuo, if he felt they kissed passionately enough. Kazuo told Sage that he did think they kissed passionately enough, but he added that he wished she'd initiate kissing more often. She replied that she'd always assumed it was the man's job to start the kiss. Then she giggled, adding, "What if you don't want to be kissed at that moment and say no?"

Kazuo laughed even harder and said, "I'll never say no to you when it comes to sex, affection, or any other form of love." Sage leaned over and gave him a passionate kiss. That immediately changed their normal for the better!

Such seemingly small romantic expressions are essential for sexual and relationship satisfaction. Unfortunately, when you live together, with all the daily hassles and challenges that entails, it's easy to let romance take a backseat. Instead of treating each other as lovers, you can become teammates handling the complex world of work, children, family, friends, and whatever the crisis of the moment might be. You may know you're not getting enough romance, but still you postpone it, waiting for a break—a vacation, holiday, or celebration—when you can be together. This postponement

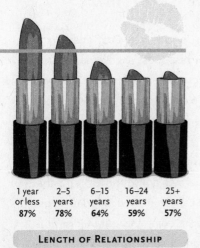

1 year or less	2–5 years	6–15 years	16–24 years	25+ years
87%	78%	64%	59%	57%

LENGTH OF RELATIONSHIP

is a common mistake. Our study shows that relationships actually need the nourishment of romance on a more frequent basis.

Don't panic if your relationship lacks romance, but do change the pattern. Play with the possibilities. Surprise each other. And put your heart into the effort.

It's especially important to create romantic surprise in your everyday life. Leave a love note on your partner's car windshield. Call at noon just to say "I love you." Share a shower at the end of the day. Romance needn't be expensive, laborious, or grandiose. Men and women of all ages describe small tokens of love as the sweetest.

Make sure, as well, that you recognize and respond to your partner's romantic overtures. Small gestures delivered with love too often are ignored or underappreciated. Notice when your partner is tidying up the sink to please you, or brings you a cup of tea when you're feeling cold. Acknowledge the gift. It means a lot more if that extra hug is also reciprocated. And if you pay close attention, you may find you have more romance in your life than you thought.

Tool 5 ▶ Rules of the Game

There's a lot of game playing in romance. First one person makes a move, then the other responds. The element of surprise is important, but it's also essential that both players know the rules and agree to play by them; it's no fun if one person makes a move and the other leaves the table or starts playing a different game.

Let's say you make a move toward your partner that you think is romantic, but your partner doesn't interpret it that way. Perhaps you come home early to make a nice dinner, but because you don't *say* that you're doing this out of love, your partner just doesn't get the connection. You feel a little hurt, right? But what if it's just a misunderstanding over the rules of the game? Your partner might be one of those people who respond better to verbal moves than to nonverbal ones—who need to hear the words "I love you" before they're sure they're loved.

Too many of us show love in the way we'd like to receive it, without taking into account our partners' needs and preferences. So before you make your first move, make sure you and your partner both understand and agree upon the rules. Don't be afraid to ask what your partner finds romantic. Talk about it, and share your own desires. Get curious and find out where your preferences differ, why you find some of the same things romantic and others not so much.

Remember that some gender differences are normal. Women in our study said they like to be kissed and told *in unique and surprising ways* how much they are loved. Men said their favorite romantic moments are when they give and receive physical affection and are making love. Significantly, most men also are dissatisfied with the amount of affection and attention they normally receive. Contrary to the stereotype of men as indifferent to romance, the Normal Bar showed most men to be equally or even *more* needy for expressions of romance than women are. Keep this in mind as you sort out the rules of the game that will keep you both engaged.

If you or your partner is unsure about what you want or expect, then talk about your fondest and most romantic moments so far. If you can't think of any romantic moments that stand out in your relationship, talk about the romantic scenes that have impressed you in books and movies. Discuss ways for each of you to bring more romance into the relationship.

Then start playing. Make a romantic move toward your partner, and see what happens. One move at a time, and you both win.

TOOL 6 ▶ The Three-Prong Romance Test

When bringing romance back into your relationship or increasing the level of romance, be sure you use the "three-prong standard." These three prongs are the core elements you need to make a romantic connection between you and your partner.

PRONG 1 ▷ TRUE EXPRESSION OF YOUR LOVE

Be genuine. We often toss off "I love you" in passing or at the end of phone calls. But to create a deep connection, it has to be said with focus and intention, in a way that emotionally touches your partner.

PRONG 2 ▷ YOUR DEEP EMOTIONAL DESIRE TO CONNECT

Be present emotionally. Your words are not as important as the shared knowledge that you are together and you want to share what's on your mind and in your heart, for now and for the future.

PRONG 3 ▷ ELEMENT OF MYSTERY OR SURPRISE

Be spontaneous. Romance is hugely enhanced by surprise and novelty, by discovering or experiencing something new together, especially if you both agree it's extraordinary. When you arrange an experience that your partner knows was difficult or unusual for you, that creates gratitude and love. Any action out of the "norm" counts!

Talk to your partner about the three prongs, then come up with some ideas to try together that meet the test. Here are some suggestions:

▷ Designate one night a week (or more or less, to suit a sexual frequency you both agree on) for sexual romance. This will cover Prong 1 (true expression of your love) and Prong 2 (your deep emotional desire to connect). Mutually agree if it will include going out first, candlelight, fine dining, massage, or watching a sexy or explicit movie. But don't always do the same thing. Look for ways to surprise each other (Prong 3) on Romance Night. The unexpected could be a heartfelt note or card, a love poem, more affection than usual, or just kissing your partner lightly on the neck or holding hands, if this isn't in your usual norm.

▷ Talk about the words of love you like to hear, and how often you need to hear them (Prong 2—your deep emotional desire to connect). Would you like to say "I love you" at the end of every telephone conversation? Would it be possible to sign your e-mails or texts with "xxxox" or "ALIWansU" (All I Want Is You)? Do you need to hear "I love you" more in bed (Prong 1—true expression of your love)? Ask what your partner likes, and then, when it's unexpected (Prong 3—element of mystery or surprise), start integrating those words more into your day-to-day life.

▷ What amount and kind of time is missing? What interferes with quality time? If there isn't enough quality time, intimate gestures such as quick sex before going to sleep won't seem romantic; they may even alienate. To reverse this pattern, create an unexpected (Prong 3— element of mystery or surprise) block of time to be with your partner. Clear away the distractions (Prong 1—true expression of your love) and focus intently on what your partner is saying. Sit close and touch (Prong 2—your deep emotional desire to connect), and rediscover each other.

▷ If your partner needs a clean bedroom or help with the children before he or she can feel romantic, then these acts of service become expressions of love (Prong 1— true expression of your love). They should also be more gratifying for you when you realize what they mean to your partner (Prong 2—your deep emotional desire to connect). Such acts are especially meaningful when they break the household routine (Prong 3—element of mystery or surprise).

Tool 7 ▶ A Gift with a Twist

Never underestimate the power of romantic gifts, but remember that the gift needs to be meaningful, personal, and something the other person will enjoy. A toaster or desk organizer alone isn't going to do the trick! However, if given a romantic twist, even a practical gift can resonate with love. So, for example, if you are going to give that desk organizer, let it open to a few sheets of love poems. Or put an IOU in the toaster for three breakfasts in bed! And if you want to start improving your sex life, look for romantic gifts around birthdays, anniversaries, or vacations that will promote passion as well as love.

Tool 8 ▶ Block Dating Tip

The Normal Bar shows that date nights are essential for most couples' happiness, but not everyone with children can afford a sitter. What to do? Consider block dating. Find other families on your block or in your building and get to know them! If they have kids the same age, that's ideal. Even if it's just one family, you can trade child care. Every other week, you'll take their kids so they can go out for the evening, then they do the same for you. The whole neighborhood will be happier!

CHAPTER 4

Shows of Affection

"I just read public affection is making a comeback."

R emember those moments in middle school or high school when the girl or boy you had a crush on first touched you? Most teenagers *live* for moments like that. They flirt and touch and kiss for the thrill and anticipation of it. After they finally have sex, however, the fun of just being excited by lips and hands and each other's closeness becomes secondary. Instead of enjoying proximity and the promise of a kiss, they get frustrated and perhaps resentful if affectionate embraces don't lead fairly quickly to sex. Some accuse their partners of teasing or "holding out" on them, and may even break up with them. But for many teenagers, sex is put off for quite a long time, and the kissing and touching is what keeps them together. Affection may not have the sizzle of sex, but it can give a relationship staying power, especially if its importance is appreciated by both partners.

Adults still get the puppy love feeling early in a relationship. They, too, kiss and cuddle, sitting on each other's laps, holding hands, nuzzling, and giving each other love pats. Then they progress to sexual intimacy, which ideally stays satisfying for a very long time. If other aspects of the relationship also stay strong, the couple will feel intensely connected. But even in sexually satisfying relationships, gestures of simple affection play a valuable supporting role.

Affection is not sophisticated. It's not sexy or steamy. But when it falters, the relationship loses a core source of strength.

What Kinds of Affection Do People Share?

We've all seen young couples who are so connected that their bodies lean against each other, their fingers intertwine, and they can't tear their eyes away from each other. Sometimes their affection and desire are so palpable that their friends will say, only half kidding, "Get a room!" But they don't always need a room. The point, at times, is to display their affection, to announce it to the world, and share their pride and joy. Public shows of affection allow these couples to demonstrate to each other how in love they are, and also to reinforce the romantic bond outside of the bedroom.

Now try to think of the last time you saw older, more established couples displaying that kind of affection toward one another. We aren't talking about passionate or lascivious groping. We're thinking of couples who embrace each other, hold hands, gently touch each other, or give each other an occasional peck on the cheek—who use affectionate gestures in public to reinforce their private feelings of intimacy and love. Our suspicion was that these gestures are *not* the norm among long-term couples, and we wondered what effect the presence or absence of such public displays actually has on relationships.

How often do people display public affection (hugging, hand-holding, caressing, and kissing)?

Generally speaking, 40% of all respondents told us they never or rarely engage in public caressing, hand-holding, kissing, or hugging. Only 13% said they show affection publicly at least once a week. And there was virtually no difference between men and women on this one.

Does age matter? Yes, younger people are more likely to show affection in public, but by a smaller margin than you might think. Nearly a quarter of men and women aged 18 to 24 said they never or hardly ever show any kind of public affection. That compares to 37% of our 35-to-44-year-olds—not a huge gap! However, the gap widens with age. Among those 45 and older, 49%—nearly half—of all men and women have stopped showing any sort of public affection.

Now, there are several possible reasons for these findings. Some in the older generations grew up in eras when *all* public displays of affection were discouraged. Others may have grown more conservative with age. It could also be that older couples feel censored by our current society. One couple, both aged 65, told us about their very discouraging experience just a couple of years ago on New Year's Eve.

PUBLIC AFFECTION
WINNER: SPAIN

62% of couples in Spain display public affection several times a week!

They'd gone to a fancy and expensive restaurant where the superb food and special wines had them feeling exuberantly affectionate. From time to time they gave each other a kiss, which they described as not quite passionate but a "tad more than affectionate." Before they knew it, the maître'd approached them and said such behavior wasn't allowed. Chastened, they stopped, but they were very irritated at the scolding—and astounded to be told that kissing on New Year's Eve was considered inappropriate!

We thought we might see more public expression of affection among lesbian couples, given that women generally hug and kiss their friends more in public than men do. Perhaps female same-sex couples express more public affection in the comfort zone of the gay community? Nope. In general, lesbian public affection norms are no different from those of heterosexual couples.

Duration of the relationship does make a difference, however, especially at the ten-year mark. An average of 28% of both men and women in the first ten years of a relationship said they rarely or never display public affection. After ten years that number jumps to 49%. Time clearly takes a toll on spontaneous displays of affection!

While more than half of all couples *do* let their affection show, the trend lines are worrisome because they suggest that spontaneity declines as relationships age. They could also mean that nondemonstrative partners gradually stop noticing those small gestures, and so stop reciprocating

The No-Show Zone

After 10 years in a relationship, or at age 45, almost half of all couples stop showing affection in public.

them. But this doesn't mean the love is gone. Even long-term partners can feel rejuvenated—and reassured—by an unanticipated hug or kiss. Remember, demonstrations of affection do not need to be flamboyant or immodest to be effective. A squeeze of the hand, a touch on the neck, a hug, or just a long intense look exchanged between partners can add a vital boost of connection to an ordinary day.

How often *do couples kiss passionately?*

Sometimes a simple question opens up a whole new dialogue. Just because people say they still kiss passionately, that doesn't mean they do it often. If we add the number of people who rarely kiss passionately to the people who never do, we come up with a whopping 56% of men and women who only kiss passionately once in a blue moon, or not at all.

Abby, married for fifteen years, told us, "The thought of making out with my husband makes me want to throw up." Strange as it may sound, Abby isn't looking for a divorce. She said she loves her husband. But there are other forces working against that relationship, according to the Normal Bar.

The first is that she has children. More than half of couples who have kids told us they rarely or never passionately kiss, compared to just 35% of those who don't have kids. Children are the unintentional destroyers of romance and passion for way too many parents.

No Kissing!

56% of people said they rarely or never kiss passionately.

The second major factor that's likely undermining Abby's appetite for passionate kissing is the longevity of her relationship—fifteen years. Between ten and twenty years, 61% of couples said they rarely or never kiss passionately.

Like many other people in a long-term relationship, Abby has come to treat her marriage like a business instead of a love affair.

Couples Who Rarely or Never Kiss Passionately

1 year or less	2–5 years	6–9 years	10–20 years	21 years or more
21%	32%	43%	61%	67%

She's forgone passion and affection as a daily norm for so long that the mere idea of it actually repels her. We didn't have access to her partner but we wondered how happy he could be with a wife who turns away from his kisses. Our guess is that he's stopped trying—but we also secretly wonder if he might have turned elsewhere to experience the romance and affection that's missing at home?

That's not an idle worry. The Normal Bar suggests that the absence of passionate kisses either has a negative impact on happiness or is a sign of a relationship on the decline. Among men and women who are extremely unhappy in their relationships, 56% said they rarely or never kiss passionately, compared to only 26% of those who are extremely happy in their relationships. The majority (58%) of people who are extremely happy share a passionate kiss several times a week.

And while passionate kissing isn't a requirement for sex, it seems to be a core component of *pleasurable* sex. Among people who love having sex with their partners, 85% also kiss passionately. Among men and women who do not enjoy sex, 86% of them rarely or never kiss passionately!

Saying "I love you"

There's an old joke about a guy who wonders why his wife wants to hear that he loves her. He tells her, "Hey, I told you once, I love you. If that changes, I'll let you know!"

In reality, it's no joke. Plenty of men and women actually do think that because their partners are loved, it's not necessary to *tell* them they're loved. But the Normal Bar shows that it actually is impor-tant to say "I love you"—and often! Of those who tell their partners every day that they love them, 74% told us that they're very satisfied in their sex lives. The connection becomes even clearer when we look at general hap-piness. Among men and women who are extremely content in their overall relationship, 88% say "I love you" on a daily basis!

Our message is not that "I love you" is a magic bullet, but those three words do seem to make partners feel more secure, important, and treasured. They help to keep hearts full and let the other person know that the relationship isn't cooling or being taken for granted.

WHO PASSIONATELY KISSES MOST OFTEN?

ITALY: 75% of Italian men and women say they passionately kiss several times a week. SPAIN: a close second at 72%.

Saying "I love you" and not meaning it

The effectiveness of those magic words, of course, depends on how honestly they're delivered and how genuinely they're felt. We were a bit afraid to ask how many people say "I love you" to their partners without meaning it, but to our relief only 1% of the happiest of couples say the three magic words often without meaning them. It is a genuine expression of connection for the vast majority of happy couples.

Unhappy partners, however, are more likely to throw out empty "I love yous." More than one-fourth of our unhappy men and women admitted to saying the words without the emotion to back them up, and another 20% told us they say them without *ever* meaning them. The false "I love you" may be deployed to protect the feelings of a partner who is no longer loved, or, more sinisterly, to buy time for an impending exit from the relationship. This is a sad situation for all concerned, since the person who is giving false feedback generally feels conflicted, guilty, fake, and even hopeless, and the words will have such a hollow ring that the recipient just feels more confused and insecure because of them. Ultimately, the only "I love you" that works is the true one.

Do you compliment your partner?

How often does your partner tell you that you're handsome or beautiful? We found that 39% of all men and 24% of women have partners who hardly ever or never praise their appearance. This isn't good, and when it comes to those who *do* compliment their partners, the picture still isn't great. Only 9% of men and 18% of women said their partners tell them they look good every day. The numbers aren't much higher for weekly compliments.

The relevance of this dearth of praise became clear when we directed the question specifically to unhappy couples. Half of these men and 38% of women said their partners never compliment them on their looks. And among those who are very dissatisfied with their sex lives, the correlation

INTERNATIONAL
CHECKPOINT

Only 24% of men and women in China said their partners tell them they are attractive every day or a couple times a week.

was even more profound, with 85% of sexually dissatisfied men and 52% of women saying their partners never praise their appearance.

But looks are only one measure of attractiveness, so we asked the same question about various other assets a person might feel proud of, including intelligence. Unfortunately, the results were virtually the same. Couples are just not stroking each other's egos very much. And why not? A few compliments would be so easy to dispense, and yet the majority of our respondents are denying their partners the pleasure of praise.

Cuddling

Ask people who've just ended a long-term relationship what they miss most, and many will describe the body contact, the snuggling and cuddling that made them feel intimately connected. This makes sense. Close skin-to-skin contact is a primal need. Yet globally 35% of men and women rarely or never cuddle or hold each other! Fortunately, there is at least one haven for cuddlers. In Spain a huge percentage reported that they cuddle at least several times a week. Maybe the phrase Latin Lovers should be changed to Latin Cuddlers! Affection reigns in Spain.

We aren't being overly romantic about the importance of cuddling and holding each other close. Only 6% of noncuddlers are sexually satisfied, and only 11% of them said that they're happy with their relationships.

> INTERNATIONAL CHECKPOINT
>
> 77% of couples in Spain say they cuddle several times a week!

Some of these people just don't want to get close to their partners, but the Normal Bar suggests, once again, that for others, children could be getting in the way. While a whopping 82% of childless partners cuddle regularly, only 68% of parents do. That disparity suggests that couples with children may be sacrificing their own vital snuggling and cuddling time. It's hard to be sensual with a three-year-old between you and a baby crying in the next room. Also, many parents get so caught up in cuddling and tending their kids that they forget their partners also need to be held. Bring some of that vital body contact back to each other!

Pet names

Sound silly? Maybe, but people like pet names such as Honey, Babe, and Sweetheart! These names are used by 65% of our respondents, and nearly half of the others told us they wish their partners would use them. These names resonate with intimacy and affection, and some are also sexy. One couple told us they make up new names for each other almost every night—a game of playful ardor. Another told us that for eleven years they would only call each other by their first name—until the day they overheard another couple call each other "Sweetheart," and the husband told his wife that he wished she would sometimes call him by an endearment. It didn't take long to integrate this new normal into the relationship and they both really enjoy being addressed as "Sweetie" and "Honey." This small change made them both feel a little bit more beloved.

Surprisingly, pet names appear to make a noteworthy contribution to overall happiness and sexual satisfaction in a relationship. Of the couples who are extremely happy and sexually satisfied, 76% use pet names!

Hand-holding

About three-fourths of all young heterosexual and homosexual couples, up to the age of thirty-five, hold hands. Yet after thirty-five, just over half of couples in every age group still hold hands. And the longer a couple has been together, the less likely they are to link hands.

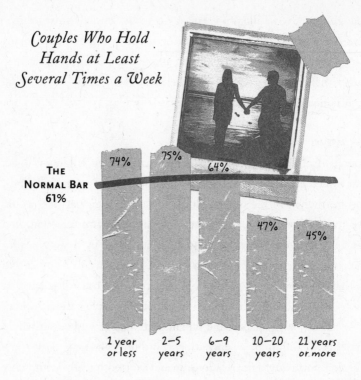

Couples Who Hold Hands at Least Several Times a Week

THE
NORMAL BAR
61%

74% 75% 64% 47% 45%

1 year   2–5   6–9   10–20   21 years
or less   years   years   years   or more

Most couples hold hands often in their first five years together, but things start to change around year six. That drop-off is significant (11%) but not as dramatic as the plunge after ten or more years, when more than half of couples no longer hold hands. These people are letting go of a valuable way to bond, repair, and communicate support and affection.

If you doubt this, consider the now classic study conducted at the University of North Carolina, in which researchers put two random groups of couples in different rooms and wired them up with heart monitors and other medical devices to gauge the benefits of hand-holding. The only difference between the two groups was that one set of couples was told to hold hands while working through an argument and the others were seated individually. The couples holding hands showed much less mental and physical stress (even lowered blood pressure). This suggests that hand contact could be especially important when a serious dispute arises. But don't wait for a crisis; make hand-holding part of your normal now.

No Touching?

The following ethnicities say they never *hold hands:*

African Americans: 39%
Hispanics: 19%
Whites: 17%
Asians: 13%

New Normal Advice

Caitlin and Eli had been married for eleven years when they became concerned that intimacy and romance were slipping away from their relationship. So, after reviewing some of our early data on cuddling and hand-holding, they decided to change their normal.

Caitlin was thirty-eight, Eli forty-three, and they had an eight-year-old son, Danny, whose weekly basketball games at the local YMCA they attended along with some thirty other families. They noticed at these games that none of the other parents ever seemed to cuddle, hold hands, or hug. Even though it wasn't "normal" for them, either, they decided to challenge this group norm. With intention, they walked into the Y holding hands or linking arms. When there weren't enough seats, Caitlin would sit on Eli's lap with her arm around him. She gave him occasional kisses on the neck, and

Eli would rub Caitlin's back. They wondered if this would embarrass Danny, but he was clearly glad to see his parents happy. Only the other couples stared. Eli and Caitlin found this amusing. They liked their new normal a lot.

Sharing more affectionate displays made them feel not only more connected but also younger. They found their playful kisses and nuzzles rekindled a sense of romance. And introducing more affection into their relationship helped them lighten up together, flirt and laugh more. This created a ripple effect through all their interactions. Hand-holding and cuddling changed the way they looked at each other and enhanced their mutual attraction. They felt lucky to retrieve this vital part of being lovers and realized how much they'd denied the relationship by giving up the thrill of holding, touching, and kissing each other—wherever they were.

Meanwhile, they set a new tone and example for those other parents at the Y. Some watching Caitlin and Eli might have thought, *Who do they think they are, carrying on like that?* Some might have speculated, *Those two must be dating or just married!* But others were surely envious because a dramatic change soon came over the whole crowd. By the end of the three-month basketball season, the bleachers were full of cuddling couples!

It may feel awkward to reactivate physical behavior that's gone by the wayside, but once jump-started, it's easy to continue. And as an added bonus, when you change your own normal, you just might inspire others to change theirs.

TOOL 9 ▶ Let's Bring Back the Make-Out Session!

Have you stopped kissing passionately when you make love? If so, it's time to talk about it. Bring it up as a mutual issue when you're alone and relaxed. Talk about the importance of bringing back that early thrill of enjoying each other through kissing. If it's uncomfortable in the beginning, make it a game. Say you have to kiss for a full three minutes—and set your alarm clock to keep yourselves honest! The game might also include a ban on any serious foreplay or intercourse that's not preceded by a make-out session.

Tool 10 ▶ You Look Good

Everybody needs compliments, so never hesitate to tell your partner how great he or she looks—or how smart, clever, witty, or lovable he or she is, either. Don't worry about the phrasing, just be honest. "I saw you when I walked in the room and you looked so handsome" or "I could never have figured that out the way you did." Once you start, other compliments will come more easily. You'll be rewarded by your partner's pleasure as well as by kisses and hugs.

Tool 11 ▶ Take My Hand or I'll Take Yours

It's never too late to start holding hands again. Make an agreement to take each other's hand whenever you go out together. As a game, give yourselves just five minutes after you walk out the door to start holding hands. The first person who grabs the other one's hand wins a dollar that goes into a jar in the kitchen. If you both grab at the same time, no one pays. Use the dollars in the jar at the end of the month to reward yourselves with a special date—during which you hold hands!

Tool 12 ▶ The Power of Touch

Touching is a very powerful tool to connect with your partner in more ways than one. When your partner massages your neck or back, it not only feels wonderful, but it also keeps that much needed connection between you going strong. Physical touch can also be a tool of persuasion. Say you want to watch a movie that's a chick flick and your partner hates chick flicks, how can you break this stalemate? Try offering to rub your partner's back or shoulders for "x" amount of time while the movie is playing. You'll get to watch the movie you want and your partner gets to enjoy a little special attention. Maybe take turns picking movies and exchanging back or shoulder rubs, or take turns caressing or massaging each other while the movie is playing.

CHAPTER 5

Let's Get Physical—
Maybe Even Kinky

"Honey . . . I thought you were just going
to schedule in our date night!"

S *ex.* Tune in to any television program, open most magazines, glance up at most billboards, or Google the word "sex," and you'll find explicit pictures and stories of lust, passion, or infidelity, all featuring erotically charged men and women. Most people's sex lives, of course, are far more mundane. Real sex has to be managed in the midst of hectic schedules, family duties, household chores, and the psychological stresses of earning a living. This doesn't make it any less vital, however. The reason sex "sells" is because it's a basic human need—as well as a primal desire.

"Doesn't take much to keep me happy . . . all I need is sex three to four times a week and the occasional blow job."—male, 36, married 8 years, with kids

On a physiological level, sex is correlated with the production of dopamine and oxytocin, two hormones that promote love and attachment. Most couples get together initially because they turn each other on physically, and the importance of that physical connection does not go away. Over time, having sex helps us repair rifts in a relationship and reaffirm how special we are to one another.

That said, not all sex is good sex. The balance or imbalance of sex with love and intimacy can make the difference between an emotionally connected union and a perfunctory "let's get it over with" experience. What kind of sexual intimacy do people experience most of the time? Men and women overall answered almost identically. We were told by 48% of women and 43% of men that their usual sexual experience is "making love with a deep physical and emotional connection." Unfortunately, that leaves more than 50% of the population who describe their couplings in less enthusiastic terms.

How happy and unhappy couples experience sex

We looked at couple type and quality of sexual experience during the early to middle years after the honeymoon period is over. This is where we found substantial differences in how couples experienced their sex lives. Happy couples, unlike the vast majority of unhappy couples, are overwhelmingly likely to describe their sexual contact as "making love" and to say that it provides a deeper physical and emotional connection. Certainly some of these couples have sex primarily to achieve orgasm, but very happy couples rarely describe it that way. This suggests that a couple's happiness and making love (as opposed to less loving intercourse) go together.

Sex drive

The Normal Bar indicates that when couples are unsatisfied with their sex lives there's often an imbalance in sex drive between the partners. Among couples who said they're extremely satisfied with their sex lives, 42% also said that both partners' sex drives are about equally matched. Only 9% of the couples who said they're *dissatisfied* sexually in the relationship said their sex drives were equally matched. Sex is clearly more enjoyable if both initiate it and mutually want it than if one partner is always doing the initiating.

Unfortunately, libido can change over time, and it's difficult to predict anyone's sex drive—including your own—over the long run. When couples first meet, it's so exciting that even partners with modest sexual appetites might feel ravenous. Over time, however, voracious desire generally mellows into a less intense need. Much of this is normal, and most couples expect their initial lusty feelings to quiet down. But if one partner's sex drive completely evaporates and the other's doesn't, this is bound to cause problems that will need to be addressed for the sake of the relationship.

When the gap is small, couples usually can work it out without the help of a professional. But if partners can't find a normal that's mutually satisfactory, the gap can destabilize the whole relationship unless they treat it seriously, and that may involve sex therapy. The most common complaint that brings couples to sex therapists is an imbalance in partners' interest in sexual activity.

Sex Acts

*"I don't have time to do the things I used to do with past lovers.
I feel stunted by my husband's lack of capability in the bedroom."*
—female, 56, married 15 years, no kids

When we talk about sex, the general assumption is that we're talking about intercourse—but that's not always the case. While intercourse is the main event for most heterosexuals, many people have plenty of other ideas and desires. What makes one person more adventurous in the bedroom than another? The answer is a complex mix of experience, culture, and self-esteem.

The media, friends, family, and religion can all play roles in shaping our sexual attitudes. Some people with negative attitudes

about sex grew up hearing that sex is evil, desire is wrong, and arousal is inappropriate until marriage (and perhaps suspect even in a committed relationship). Such attitudes are common in many cultural and religious groups that also mandate virginity before marriage and proscribe masturbation, oral sex, anal sex, and same-sex relations.

Others may grow up with more positive messages, perhaps even with parents who tell them that sensuality is a gift, but then have negative experiences that counteract these messages. An early painful sexual encounter (such as molestation, rape, or physical abuse within a sexual relationship) can do permanent damage to one's attitude toward sex. Or, if a person feels physically unworthy or deficient in some way (real or imagined), negative body image may increase sexual inhibition, even within a loving relationship.

If you've had a bad sexual experience, you may understandably steer away from acts that remind you of the experience. If you've never tried certain sexual acts, it's equally understandable if you're reluctant to try them for the first time. But what if your partner likes the very acts that make you uncomfortable?

Therapist David Schnarch, author of *Intimacy and Desire* and *The Passionate Marriage,* writes that there's always a low- and a high-desire partner. The premise of the "coevolution" program he's developed to address this imbalance is that change needs to begin with the person who wants less sex. Why? For one thing, the partner who wants more has nowhere else to go within the vows of monogamy. For another, many psychologists believe that lack of desire most often stems from lack of intimacy, self-confidence, or self-esteem. If intimacy is increased and self-confidence and self-esteem are boosted, this frequently narrows the gap of desire between two people who love each other. Add warm, secure feelings of attachment, rather than anger and insecurity, and differences in desire can be radically reduced.

If you're always up for sex and your partner isn't, it's difficult not to feel rejected. Once those rejected feelings set in, they can infect other areas of the relationship, which eventually leads to frustration and resentment. This is why it's important to talk about sex candidly, not with accusations and tears but with mutual desire to understand each other's background and feelings and to explore possible solutions.

More than half of the people we asked—63% of women and 59% of men—said they discuss sexual preferences and technique with their partners during lovemaking. Such frank (but not insensitive or cruel) conversation can help make sex more satisfying. It also can forge a stronger emotional connection.

However, not all psychologists agree that a strong connection and intimate relationship predict erotic desire. Psychoanalyst Esther Perel takes a different tack in her book *Mating in Captivity*. She writes that desire is sometimes *diminished* when the couple is in a secure, loyal, and predictable relationship. She states that romance and desire generally require surprise and perhaps even some insecurity and longing for more attention. But, of course, what most happy couples work hard to achieve is comfort with each other and a belief in the solidity of their relationship! Dr. Perel suggests that the erotic can be invigorated in comfortable couples, but to protect monogamy and still create erotic excitement some will have to more edgily explore their erotic fantasies, keep some mystery in the relationship, and perhaps venture into sexually challenging territory!

FULL DISCLOSURE

More than half of couples discuss their preferred sexual techniques while making love.

Kinky Versus Nonkinky

"I'm finally discovering my kinky side and I have become much, much happier in my relationship."—female, 43, married 17 years, with kids

Everyone has a different idea of what constitutes kinkiness. Since most Americans include oral sex in their sexual repertoire, oral sex isn't normally seen as edgy. But what about wearing a blindfold? A bunny suit? Pretty much anything you can think of (and many things you can't) is sexually intriguing to someone somewhere.

Wanna be kinky?

We found that 86% of all men and women are intrigued by having kinky sex. And while this number includes 78% of women, a whopping 94% of men said they're interested. This means that pretty much anyone who has a man for a partner can expect a positive reaction to a kinky suggestion.

> **Mind-Bending . . .**
>
> *86% of people are intrigued by the prospect of having kinky sex.*

Prudish or kinky?

At least 83% of women feel that their partners are neither too kinky nor too prudish, but "just right." Only 11% of women feel their partners are too prudish, and 6% feel their guys are too kinky.

Among men, however, the response is more muted. Thirty-nine percent of men said their partners are too prudish, and just 1% said their partners are too kinky for their taste. It's clear that a sizable number of men would like their partners to be more sexually adventurous.

"When I said we should try something new and exciting . . .
I kind of had something else in mind."

Heterosexual curiosity with bisexuality: Was it fun?
Fabulous? Or regrettable?

We reviewed thousands of open-ended answers about sexual fantasies and found that a large number of men and women fantasize about threesomes and same-sex experiences; we wondered how common it is for people to act on these fantasies. The Normal Bar shows that it's much more common for women than for men! Nearly one-fourth, or 23%, of heterosexual women have experimented with bisexuality, compared to just 13% of heterosexual men.

Other studies have shown a recent rise in same-sex sexual experimentation among younger men and women (reflected in the popularity of Katy Perry's hit song "I Kissed a Girl"), but widespread taboos seem to inhibit men more than women at every age. Most gay men, as well as most heterosexuals, believe that men are either straight or gay, or else are in denial about their true sexuality. The data, however, show that some men who have strong heterosexual desire and are committed to a heterosexual sexual identity can also enjoy sex with another man without labeling themselves bisexual. Such sexual adventures or encounters vary in personal significance. For some these are one-time experiments. For others they become a regular part of life.

Masturbation

We found that 96% of men and 82% of women masturbate. While other studies have shown the same rate as ours for men, their national average for women in the United States is closer to 50%. However, what we really wanted to know was how individuals feel about their *partner's* masturbation. Did our respondents know if their partners masturbated? Did it bother them if the partner did? It turns out that women are a lot more aware of their partners' masturbatory habits than vice versa. Eighty percent of women told us that their partners masturbate, compared to only 50% of men. And yet only 2% of these men said they're bothered that their partners masturbate, compared to 10% of these women. It seems that the women take it more personally than men do.

Should people worry if their partners masturbate?

If you masturbate, does this make your sex life more enjoyable, or less? Actually . . . it doesn't make any difference. Both men and women masturbate, whether or not they are happy with

MASTURBATION IS NORMAL

More than 80% of men and women "independently" augment even the best sex life.

their sex lives and relationships. Masturbation isn't a symptom of being sex starved, or of an alternative fantasy life, or of an affair. It is an addition to, not a substitute for, partnered sex. Men and women may feel the sexual urge when they're alone, or they may want to satisfy the urge without using all the physical and emotional energy that making love requires.

Some women told us they thought happy couples with a good sex life should not masturbate, but we found that it's normal for people to augment even the best sex life with the help of a vibrator or one's own hand. If this comes as a surprise to you, you're not alone. One woman said about our findings, "I must live in a cardboard box, because I thought people only masturbated because they weren't getting enough sex."

That common misunderstanding can cause a lot of heartache. If you feel you should meet every one of your partner's sexual needs and fantasies, and even the need for a quick unemotional orgasm, you're placing unreasonable and unnecessary demands on yourself and your relationship. Remember that masturbation doesn't drain sexual energy from a relationship: It builds it. The more someone has sexual urges and satisfies them, the more pleasurable sex becomes within the relationship. Large national studies, such as one conducted by the Social Organization of Sexuality in 1994, have shown that the more men and women masturbate, the higher the sexual frequency in their relationships.

Oral sex

The Normal Bar shows that oral sex is an American norm. We found that 91% of women in the United States give oral sex to their men, and 79% of men return the favor to women. While our figures on oral sex for both men and women are higher than some other studies' numbers, the ratio of male versus female in the active role is consistent. Women give more than they get, and this is particularly true in the studies on hooking up among young people. Why isn't it more mutual? The imbalance is not entirely due to men's reluctance to give oral sex to women; some women are reluctant to receive it.

An additional question about oral sex is one that researchers rarely ask, unless they are studying the spread of disease: *Do women swallow semen as part of the sex act and, if they do, how does this part of the sex act affect their own and their partners' pleasure?* The answer: More than half of women do swallow semen while performing oral sex, and out of that 52%, only 9% said they don't like to do it. Still, a large minority of women do not swallow semen, and for some of them the prospect is not just unappealing but *extremely* unappealing.

Orgasms!

Wait a minute, how can this be? Only 65% of men and 67% of women find it extremely important for their partners to have an orgasm! Perhaps we should look to France for guidance, since the number of respondents who care about their partners' orgasm is much higher in France than elsewhere. But why don't *all* lovers want their partners' sexual experience to be orgasmic?

Perhaps our respondents recognize that sex involves more than an orgasm and that the most important thing is to make each other feel good and well loved. But these results also could reflect complacency on the part of couples. While having an orgasm is important to women and correlates with

> **INTERNATIONAL CHECKPOINT**
>
> 73% of men in France said it's extremely important to them that their partners have an orgasm.

sexual satisfaction and relationship happiness, most women don't always expect to climax, so men may assume that women don't need or want to orgasm every time they make love—or even frequently. At the same time, many men don't even count a sexual experience as intercourse *unless* they ejaculate, so it's sobering that over a third of women don't care whether their men come or not. Some part of this response for both men and women may indicate selfishness, and that's never good in any relationship.

It's worth remembering that intercourse is not the only path to orgasm. Most partners (78%) bring a partner to a climax at least some of the time just by touching. And only 4% of people who have sex this way consider it unsatisfying.

THE POWER OF TOUCH

81% of women and 76% of men sometimes reach orgasm by being touched . . . without *intercourse.*

The sensation of being touched is different enough from intercourse that some people like to vary their sex lives by touching their partners to orgasm even when intercourse is possible. It might also be the main sexual technique in relationships when one or the other partner is unable to have intercourse or finds that intercourse, while pleasant, provides ineffective stimulation. Then touching turns into a primary option.

Anal sex

Perhaps the most difficult sex act to talk about is anal sex. Because of the obvious associations, the anus isn't generally considered to be a sexual organ. But, in fact, it is a highly sensitive and, for some, erotically charged part of the body that's used for sex play by both heterosexuals and homosexuals. About a quarter of our couples have tried anal intercourse and a good number of them find it satisfying. Of those who have tried it, just 6% of women and 2% of men don't like it. One contributing factor in these cases might be lack of preparation.

Anal sex is one of the few sex acts you have to learn how to do. Without adequate skill or care, the insertion of a penis or even a finger into the anus can be extremely painful and tear sensitive tissues. There also are health dangers associated with harmful bacteria in this part of the body, which can get into the bloodstream. And anal sex raises the risk of AIDS transmission. Perhaps because of the potential for discomfort and the need for careful hygiene, it's not a common sexual act in the United States.

People who don't like anal sex, or don't want to even try it, say they don't think anything to do with defecation is sexy, and they don't want to learn to do anything that could make the transmission of disease more likely. So why *would* anyone perform anal sex? Because when it's done right, it's arousing. Sometimes when a woman or man is extremely turned on, there is an urge to be entered anally. The anus is tighter than a vagina and men often love the added friction. Some women say when they are extremely aroused, they can't tell the difference between a penis being in the vagina or anus, and they like the additional stimulation.

INTERNATIONAL CHECKPOINT

In France and Italy, anal sex is much more widely accepted because of its long history as a means of birth control. It's also viewed as a way to preserve virginity in Catholic countries (according to the letter of the law, if not exactly the spirit of it). In these countries the association between anal sex and homosexuality may be less prevalent than in the United States.

Most countries we surveyed are right in line with the United States when it comes to **ANAL SEX**, except for France and Italy: **46%** of couples in **FRANCE** and **45%** of couples in **ITALY** practice anal sex.

Many women in the United States (as well as male partners in same-sex relationships) told us they tried it, found it too painful, and that was that. However, when we looked at our couples who are happiest, we found that 35% of them have practiced anal sex! Probably it's the sexual adventurer in them: let no act pass uninvestigated!

Sexual positions

While the missionary position is the most common sexual position, it's not what most men prefer. It turns out that men's favorite position, coming in at 40% on the Normal Bar is . . . doggie style. Second position, favored by 24% of men, is to be on the bottom with their partners on top. So why is the missionary position considered most normal?

Probably because 30% of women prefer it. Another 24% of women prefer being on top. However, plenty of other more creative positions were mentioned, including:

MOST DESIRABLE SEXUAL POSITIONS

Doggie style was the winner among MEN, even internationally.

Among WOMEN internationally, it was a toss-up between the missionary position and woman on top.

"At right angles to each other, my legs over his butt, his torso perpendicular to mine." —female, 51, divorced, in a 1-year domestic partnership, no kids

"Him kneeling up and me half on my front, half on my side with one leg between his and the other outside." —female, 23, never married, dating seriously for 1 year, no kids

"Doggie bagging: When you are simultaneously doing doggie style and tea bagging your partner. This requires her to be very flexible

and bend 180 degrees at the waist so that her mouth is near her own vagina."—male, 27, never married, in a 2-year relationship, no kids

"Her on back with legs on my shoulders."—male, 42, in a 16-year domestic partnership, with kids

"I like when he holds my legs separately open and sucking my breast a lot when he enters me."—female, 31, married 6 years, with kids

"I'm lesbian; there is no 'position' for us!"—female, 51, divorced, in a 2-year relationship, no kids

"He's lying down, and I ride him, Yee-ha!"—female, 49, married 14 years, with kids

"Her on top, also doing the 69 thing, however, we can't do that anymore because my wife is letting herself go."—male, 52, married 26 years, with kids

"Me on top, with her knees pinned to her ears."—male, 36, married, with kids

"Sitting up in bed with her on top and my face in her chest; alternatively, walking around with her riding in front."—male, 34, married 8 years, with kids

For all this creativity, however, no one particular position seemed to correspond with more sexual or relationship satisfaction.

Sex toys

If you aren't well acquainted with vibrators, it might surprise you to know that they've become very popular. Not so long ago, studies on sexuality found that fewer than 20% of women used vibrators. Today, more than half of all couples include at least one partner who uses a sex toy—and that number is expected to climb. Many Walmarts now sell vibrating "cock rings" right in the condom section, and online stores like Drugstore.com sell a wide variety of devices such as dildos, vibrators, textured condoms, and other sexual paraphernalia. Big-time manufacturers of condoms, such as Trojan, have whole lines of vibrators and plan to increase their production in this area. Why? Because so many people buy them. The market for these toys seems to be insatiable.

Uses Sex Toys with Partner

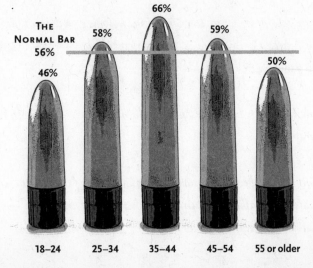

THE NORMAL BAR 56%

| 18–24 | 25–34 | 35–44 | 45–54 | 55 or older |

46% 58% 66% 59% 50%

Our data show that a majority of couples use them in every age group *except* between the ages of 18 and 24. It may be that the youngest group is a little unsure about using a sex toy while still learning how to be comfortable with sex in general and partnered sex in particular.

While the Normal Bar reflects the widespread acceptability and presence of these devices, it is still true that 13% of women and 8% of men are bothered if their partners use a sex toy. One young woman said she thought it was "pitiful" that anyone "needed" a sex toy. Others criticized their use as impersonal and selfish. Some said they'd feel rejected if they knew their partners used a sexual aid—even if the toy was used only when they were not in town. We hope these people will be reassured by our findings that using sex toys has no overall impact on a relationship's happiness or sexual satisfaction.

New Normal Advice

Jason and Stella had been married for eighteen years when Stella read some of our Normal Bar data on sexual satisfaction and, for the first time, felt emboldened to ask her husband to name his number-one sexual fantasy. But she was stunned when he responded that he didn't have one! Stella asked why not. Jason said he used to fantasize about having sex with his wife in different positions and using sex toys, but he became frustrated knowing that Stella would never try anything new, so he stopped setting himself up for disappointment. This made Stella very sad. She thought they still had great sex, and she enjoyed making love with her husband. But she had to admit that Jason was right, they'd been making love virtually the same way since they first met, with only minor variations.

Even though Stella was happy with their sex life, she was open to trying some new positions or sex toys. But Jason didn't want to ask her to do something she wasn't comfortable with, and they were both uncertain how to proceed. So, to help them begin the process of changing their normal, we shared the following metaphor:

Imagine that your partner opens a fine Italian restaurant, and you open a high-end steak house. You eat at each other's restaurants every day, feeling satisfied and happy, and at first you have no desire to go anywhere else. But what if you and your partner never change your menus? After a few years, one or both of you might be tempted or curious about other restaurants.

It's the same with sex. Variety adds necessary spice. Even the addition of a small appetizer can open up new flavors. Jason said he was just looking for a little side dish once in a while, but he was thrilled to learn that Stella was open to a daily special! That's all it took. They didn't need a whole new menu.

Adding a few new items might be all you and your partner need to enjoy each other more, too. How do you add these items? Describe the various possibilities that you each have considered and discuss what you both feel comfortable adding. Best way to do this? Use *The Normal Bar* as a tool for communication.

Start off with "Honey, did you know . . ." and use one of the data points from this book. Using information as a conversation starter is an easy way to open up a conversation without implying any personal criticism of your own practices. Once you're discussing our more provocative suggestions, it will feel natural to talk about trying them yourselves. Remember our story of the woman who asked her husband if he felt they were kissing passionately enough? She only asked that because of the data from the Normal Bar, but as a result, their relationship was enhanced. So talk about your "restaurant" with your partner and open up the possibilities that you'd feel comfortable adding to your sexual menu.

TOOL 13 ▶ I Want "_____" in Bed Game

In her book *Talk Sexy to the One You Love,* sex therapist Barbara Keesling suggests a verbal game to boost sexual communication. Each person has to think of five sexual acts to do or receive in bed, using one of these formats or something similar: *I want you to **VERB** your **NOUN ADJECTIVE** or **ADVERB*** or this one: *I want to **VERB** your **NOUN ADJECTIVE** or **ADVERB**.* Try this with you partner using these examples as inspiration:

> *I want you to thrust your penis deeply.*
> *I want you to insert your finger gently.*
> *I want to bite your naked shoulder a little.*
> *I want to feel your passionate kisses hard and long.*
> *I want to stroke your sexy body gently.*
> *I want to kiss your beautiful breasts softly.*
> *I want to grab your butt roughly.*
> *I want to hear your sexiest fantasies uncensored.*
> *I want to kiss your neck lightly.*

TOOL 14 ▶ Get Kinky with It—Blindfold!

What about using a blindfold so that you can't see what your partner is going to do to you (or vice versa)? As you sit expectantly in darkness, your partner might stroke you from head to toe, surprising you. When it's your turn, touch your blindfolded partner with sensual fabrics, such as a feather, silk, cashmere, or a boa. All your senses are keener when one of them is deprived, so touch will be even more exciting than usual.

Tool 15 ▶ Get Kinky with It—Surprise!

Women: Wear a skirt and go out to dinner without wearing underwear. Casually mention this as you are leaving the house, and the evening will instantly get a charge. Then let your partner touch your leg from time to time (of course, you could be even more daring—but that could get you arrested). Usually just this little tease is enough for an extra-intense session at bedtime.

Tool 16 ▶ Get Kinky with It—Under Arrest!

Try "cuffs"—both of you! A little restraint goes a long way. Get the Velcro type of handcuff so that you don't hurt your wrists when your partner cuffs you to the bed or cuffs your hands behind you (in a comfortable way). Think of the cuffed person as the sex captive who has to do what he or she is told. Of course, do this only in a committed relationship with someone you really trust!

Tool 17 ▶ Get Kinky with It—Exploring a Sex Shop

Today's sex shops look more like Nordstrom than like sleaze shops. Shops like Lovers in Seattle, Eve's Garden in New York, Good Vibrations in San Francisco, and Fascinations in Denver are well lit, beautifully laid out, and staffed by knowledgeable young people (usually women) who will make you feel comfortable discussing what level of vibration you might like or the newest innovation in lubricants. Go with your partner and let the store give you a tour, then pick out a few things together that tickle your imagination. Even if your choices produce more giggles than moans, you'll be happy you shopped there together.

Tool 18 ▶ Get Kinky with It—Watching a Sex Video

Explicit films used to be made only for men. But if you look at the films of Candida Royalle or peruse the catalog of goodvibrations.com you can now find movies with a bit more plot and fantasies that appeal to women, too. There are videos for same- and opposite-sex couples, and some that are educational—but still sexy. Remember that if the movie is at all erotically appealing, you will probably need to watch only about five minutes of it before you shift your attention from the screen to each other!

Tool 19 ▶ Jedi Mind Trick

If you want something done differently, try this technique: Do to your partner what you would like done to you. For example, let's say that you'd like to be touched a certain way, or perhaps you want to be held more roughly in bed. Without saying anything, treat your partner the way you'd like to be handled. If it's out of your norm, it won't go unnoticed. Then ask if your partner likes it. If so, say, "Show me how it feels."

The tools above are just a few suggestions to get you started. The main point is that breaking out of your comfort zone, however little or infrequently, can add some extra zip to most relationships. The resources listed at the end of this book will give you additional ideas.

PART

II

Living Together

CHAPTER 6

The Great Communicators

"He never listens or gives me his undivided attention."
"You have it now . . . and I'm listening."

When we asked couples to name the most fulfilling thing about their relationships, *communication* won by a mile! More than a third of both men and women ranked it first, well ahead of friendship. They also offered comments such as:

"My partner and I have similar goals and values. We work well together and can support each other. We both listen well and are willing to make adjustments as situations demand. Plus I love her more than I can put into words." —male, 33, in a 3-year relationship, no kids

"We communicate well, and when there is conflict we are able to resolve the problem. I feel that I am one of the most important things in his life and I feel the same way about him." —female, 30, in a 2-year relationship, no kids

"My girlfriend is my best friend, with whom I have the most fun, laugh the most, and have the best sex I've ever had." —male, 33, in a 1-year relationship, no kids

"We've been married for 27 years, and it just seems to keep getting better, more intimate, more romantic." —male, 65, married, with kids

"We are best friends, passionate lovers; we focus on communication and make a point of making time for each other." —female, 42, married 21 years, with kids

"We've a balance, a family; and it fits. We laugh a lot, we gossip, we go out every week on a date!" —female, 44, married 23 years, with kids

Equally resounding, recently divorced singles named lack of communication as the number-one reason why their relationships had ended. What explains this? It's simple. We all need to be heard and understood. We all need someone with whom it's safe, fun, and exciting to talk—and someone we can trust to give us honest but also compassionate feedback, who will listen and really "get" us, and vice versa. Communication is the gateway not only to important emotions but also to physical compatibility. If you want something more—or less—from your partner, then you need to feel free to express that desire, and you need for the message to be accurately received. That's communication.

Who communicates best?

When we asked men and women if they thought they communicated well in their relationships, 90% of men and 92% of women rated themselves as good to great communicators. Not bad! But perhaps people were being overly confident.

The Happiest Couples Say the Most Fulfilling Thing About Their Relationship Is . . .

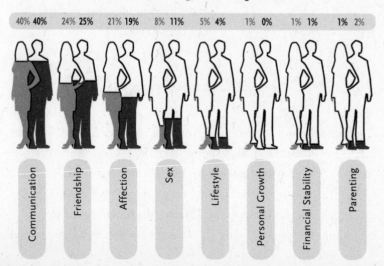

Communication	Friendship	Affection	Sex	Lifestyle	Personal Growth	Financial Stability	Parenting
40% 40%	24% 25%	21% 19%	8% 11%	5% 4%	1% 0%	1% 1%	1% 2%

When we asked women if they consider their *partners* to be good communicators, 30% said no way! And one-fourth of men said they are very dissatisfied with their partners' communication skills.

So, which group is better communicators—men or women? In general, other research gives the nod to women, but in our study, men and women assess each other's abilities almost equally. It's really too close to say, especially because so many people think they communicate well . . . and the Normal Bar tells us otherwise!

THE BEST COMMUNICATORS: SAME-SEX COUPLES!

78% of gay men and lesbians said their partners *do a great job of communicating.*

96% said they themselves *do a great job of communicating!*

The complexities of couple communication involve physical, emotional, and verbal cues that many of us have difficulty sending and receiving—for a wide variety of reasons. Because communication is such a vital element for relationship endurance and satisfaction, we thought it worth delving into these complexities on a deeper level.

Communication Devices

Technology is a modern relationship reality. Only 8% of our respondents said they never text or e-mail their partners. Another 9% said they rarely do; which leaves 83% who text and e-mail their partners a lot! Digital communication is especially normal among couples in the United States. But is that a good thing?

The jury is still out on whether technology has helped

"How was your day?"
"Fine. Yours?"

communication in relationships, or is killing it. On the one hand, people can stay in touch more easily. On the other, most communication is now in such short bits and bytes that not much is being communicated. A text message is easy to misunderstand, which can spark a needless argument. Furthermore, texting replaces a good deal of conversation that would be more bonding than "CU2nite."

This doesn't even take into account some of the major relationship offenders, such as checking e-mail while your partner is talking to you, texting during a dinner date, or canceling time together because of e-mail that's accumulated during the day and "must" be answered. As one woman told us, "It's like people are constantly wanting to be in touch with somebody other than the person in the room."

It's true: Behavior that in the past would have been coded as rude or downright hostile is now viewed as normal, thanks to technology. Social commentators worry that we are too distracted to be good companions, and also that we share so much during the day in texts, e-mails, and Skype messages, by the time we get home we're

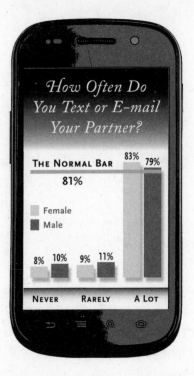

done sharing. While communication technology keeps couples much more closely in touch over long physical distances, the overall impact actually increases emotional distance. Given how important communication is for intimacy and understanding, we've got to work against these devices to keep connections real.

Communication Styles

Most people like to talk, which is great as long as they also know how to listen. Research shows that a balance in sharing airtime indicates a balance throughout the relationship. An easy flow of talking and listening is a diagnostic for happiness.

One thing that undermines good communication is the desire, on the part of one partner or both, to win or score points rather than listen, exchange opinions, and come to a mutual understanding. Communication needs to be collaborative, not competitive. Think of the goal as excellent cooperation—a win-win outcome rather than an upset.

Who interrupts more?

Nobody likes to be interrupted when telling a story or sharing thoughts. It's not just impolite, but also can be experienced as personally disrespectful. Which gender is the biggest offender when it comes to interrupting? Both are! Exactly 59% of men and 59% of women said that they're interrupted by their partners anywhere from sometimes to all the time.

Other studies have found that it's OK to interrupt, as long as both partners interrupt about equally. If only one person talks a lot and only one person gets to interrupt, that's when the quality of the relationship is diminished. But this does not mean that interruption is ever really *good* for a relationship. We found that people are twice as likely to be unhappy in their relationships if they are often interrupted by their partners. Interruptions can be especially infuriating if they're a mode of control (the interrupted person never gets a chance to finish a statement). They can signal the loss of an intimate or even civil partnership.

Fortunately, most interruptions are just an excess of zeal about a point, and the habit can be corrected by stating the obvious: "You interrupted me AGAIN! Honey, can I just finish my point? I want you to hear what I'm thinking!"

How often do you laugh at what your partner says?

One of the women we surveyed, a thirty-four-year-old mother, shared with us this personal story: She had just gotten off the phone with a friend and sat down to help her three kids with their homework, when her eight-year-old son said to her, "Why do you laugh all the time when you're talking to your friends . . . and we never see you laugh with Daddy?" She tried to remember the last time she'd laughed with her husband—and couldn't. This was a big wake-up call.

Laughing with your partner lets them know that you're fully engaged and enjoying time with them. (It also reassures the kids that their parents love and enjoy each other!) We hoped the Normal Bar would show that our couples are taking the time to enjoy each other, and laughing together is a clear sign they are. We found that 66% of couples laugh together often or all the time. In England the number is even higher—maybe it's that dry British wit, or perhaps the English have a particular communication style that promotes laughter.

WHO LAUGHS THE MOST?

70% of couples in England say they laugh often or all the time!

What isn't so funny is the big shift in laughing we see when couples hit the ten-year mark. Only 4% rarely or never laugh with their partners if they've been together nine years or less, but after ten years, 15% of couples stop laughing. If you're in a long-term relationship and have lost your sense of humor, consider using the tools at the end of this chapter to bring some laughs back into the household.

Is bickering over little things a part of your relationship?

Nobody enjoys bickering, yet no group escapes it. Regardless of age, gender, presence or absence of kids, sexual orientation, and even relationship longevity, half of our couples told us they bicker about the little things.

Arguments are not just unavoidable but necessary and even valuable as long as they lead to resolution, but bickering is the kind of small-scale arguing, repetitive nit-picking, usually over trivial matters, that never leads to resolution. With bickering, the underlying issues and comments in dispute keep resurfacing.

Psychologists have concluded that this failure or inability to resolve problems takes a toll on troubled relationships. It's when couples never can come to any agreement that relationships blow up. Endless bickering usually indicates a history of mutual frustration that keeps partners going after each other. It's a destructive communication norm.

There's also a sobering connection between bickering and sex. Among those who are very dissatisfied sexually or unhappy with their relationships, 45% said they bicker often or all the time, compared to just 11% of people who are sexually satisfied and happy with their relationships. Regardless of whether the bickering precedes or follows the unhappiness in the relationship, it is a negative signal.

Heated arguments

Heated arguments are a step up from bickering. They're impossible to ignore, and they usually revolve around major issues. For some couples, they seem to be an inescapable part of life; but, tellingly, among our happiest couples, 22% said they've *never* had a heated argument. Another 39% said heated arguments have happened occasionally over the course of the relationship, and 20% said fights happen a few times a year.

When a fight is a rare event it's not the end of the world, but 48% of unhappy couples have heated arguments either daily, weekly, or monthly. More than half don't, so overt fighting is not the root cause of unhappiness, but it is one indicator of possible trouble.

Have you ever been criticized by your partner?

If you feel like you're being criticized, chances are that your partner isn't giving you advice or feedback in a very kind or constructive way. Criticism is negative feedback that's phrased as an attack on the person instead of the problem, and not surprisingly, problems tend to fester and relationships falter when criticism becomes a "normal" communication style.

Criticizing a partner erodes the sense of trust and safety that most relationships depend on. Consider how you'd react if, instead of saying, "We've got to get this house clean," your partner called you a "slob" and asked, "Can't you ever pick up after yourself?" It's extremely unsettling when the person who's supposed to know you best calls you mediocre or witless or incompetent.

WHO'S MOST CRITICAL?

Two-thirds *of men say their women criticize them a lot, compared to* a little more than half *of women who feel criticized by their men.*

Being criticized instead of being helped and guided makes a mockery out of most wedding promises of fidelity and love, yet it seems to be difficult to avoid as the years go by. Ten years is the unhappy benchmark. After a decade together, 12% of partners say they are criticized daily—yes, *daily*! Compare this to newer relationships, where the Normal Bar for criticism is closer to 5%.

What surprised us the most was that 55% of all men who describe themselves as unhappy to slightly happy are being criticized several times a week or even daily! Looking at the bigger picture, it does appear that women are more critical of their men than men are of their women. *Two-thirds* of all men say they're criticized a lot by their partners, compared to a little more than half of women. An easy

"Oh, him? It's just easier this way; I never listen to a word he says anyway."

way to make these relationships stronger would be for both partners to channel all that critical energy into resolving the critical issues and to lay off each other over the small stuff.

Are you bossy?

Nobody likes to be bossed around; yet 45% of respondents told us their partners boss them around sometimes or all the time. This takes a toll, as we learned from the 43% of men who are very dissatisfied sexually and who consider their female partners very bossy. Significantly, only 10% of sexually satisfied men had bossy partners.

Unfortunately, bossiness gets worse with age. Only 6% of the 18-to-24-year-olds said their partners are bossy, compared to 27% of men and women aged 55 and older. Only 8% of people in new relationships described their partners as bossy, but 20% of the ten-year veterans did.

WHO'S THE BOSSIEST?

Men and women aged 55 and older are the bossiest.

Whether people change as the years go by, or partners just perceive each other differently with time, control increasingly becomes an issue for long-term couples.

Yelling

Yelling generally means that someone is out of control, angry, and aggressive—a threat. So when someone yells at you, your whole body goes into defensive mode against this emotional abuse. Words then fly in both directions that may later be regretted; but they can never be taken back.

Yelling makes a relationship toxic, and that spills into the bedroom. Over half of people who say they have bad sex lives are getting yelled at daily, several times a week, or a couple of times a month. A third of generally unhappy partners said they routinely get yelled at.

Who's doing the yelling? More women than men, by a margin of four to three. That is a substantial difference, and it probably reflects a certain restraint on the part of men who know that yelling at a woman is a major trespass. A man yelling at a woman represents more danger than vice versa because of size and strength differences between the sexes. And most men have an aptitude for violence when they are furious. Better to check the temper than risk bodily harm.

Cursing

Maybe you come from a family where swearing and insulting each other was so normal that you were conditioned to follow suit—but that still doesn't make it OK, especially not if you want a sexually satisfying and overall happy relationship. The Normal Bar shows that 90% of the happiest individuals have *never* cursed at their partners.

Among other respondents, the surprise is that men claim they're being sworn at and insulted more than women do. While 16% of women said their partners have cursed and insulted them, 21% of men said they've been the targets of their partners' swearing.

WOMEN, WATCH YOUR LANGUAGE!

21% of men said their partners curse at them from time to time, compared to only 16% of women who said their partners use nasty language.

Dealing with Conflict

All relationships have some conflict. In fact, if there seems to be *none*, the couple may be avoiding conversations they need to have to forge an intimate relationship. Therapist Felice Dunas says that good relationships swing between conflict and harmony, and a very intimate one will often swing to extremes rather than stay in a middle "safe zone" where conflict is dealt with superficially or not at all. But many couples are so afraid of conflict that they'll do anything to avoid even acknowledging a difference of opinion. This allows the differences to fester, causing continuous anger and hurt feelings. There are better solutions.

"Jim! Where are you?"

Have you ever hidden from your partner?

People need solitude for a long list of reasons. Maybe you had an argument earlier in the day and you need a "time out" to cool down, or maybe you just need some peace and silence at the end of a long day. But partners are not always understanding or cooperative when it comes to this need for solitude. That could explain why 78% of men who are in the slightly unhappy to slightly happy relationship range told us they sometimes hide from their partners.

Even among men who are extremely happy in their relationships,

38% said they search out a good hiding spot, too. Withdrawing seems to be a guy thing.

As for women, 40% said they just plain like to be by themselves from time to time; needing private alone time has nothing to do with how they feel about their partners. In other words, hiding out is not necessarily a sign of a relationship in trouble.

Who's Hiding?

78% of men who are mildly unhappy to happy said they sometimes hide from their partners.

Couch time

Ever sleep alone while your partner sleeps on the couch, or vice versa? You aren't alone. Slightly more than half of our respondents have slept separately on occasion due to a disagreement. This leads us to conclude that every home needs a couch!

Seriously, while many couples feel they've failed or are in deep trouble when one of them moves to the couch, the Normal Bar shows that this is a very common response to extreme anger: You want physical as well as psychological distance from your partner. An occasional night on the couch is no big deal. In fact, it may be the best way to get a good night's sleep without fighting through the night. It only becomes destructive if it happens night after night and turns into a form of punishment or humiliation.

But here's a heads-up: There is a small correlation between couch activity and overall happiness and sexual satisfaction. Only 1% of the happiest partners said they've ever slept on the couch, compared to 18% of *unhappy* people, who said they sleep on the couch often or all the time.

Keeping secrets

Have you ever kept a secret from your partner because you wanted to avoid conflict? If so, rest assured, others are doing it too.

In America, 43% of men and 33% of women told us they have major secrets from their partners. Even 27% of the happiest couples said they keep secrets from each other. And in France and Italy, secrets are a way of life: *Three-quarters* of these European men and women conceal intimate truths from their partners, though this may be due to cultural norms in Europe, where there's less of a premium on full disclosure. In America any significant secret between lovers is seen as a violation of intimacy.

Surprisingly, a large number of people shared their secrets with us. Maybe it felt good to unburden themselves, especially since many of the secrets involved cheating and shame. The most common secrets include emotional and physical infidelity, masturbation,

Keeps Secrets from a Partner

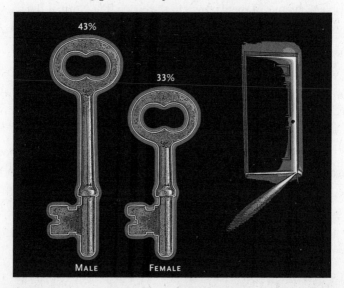

43%

33%

MALE   FEMALE

loaning money, having an abortion, being addicted to porn, and spying on partners. Also:

"I think I'm a lesbian."—female, 24, married 5 years, no kids

"My personal finances. In more debt than we'd agreed I would carry."—female, 56, married 11 years, with kids

"I'm not happy and I wish my first love would come back to me."—female, 49, married 24 years, with kids

"I have continued a relationship with another woman that I had started before I met my partner."—male, 62, divorced, dating seriously for 6 months, with kids

INTERNATIONAL CHECKPOINT

75% of men and women in **France** and **Italy** keep secrets from their partners.

"I fake orgasms. All the time. But it's really not him, it's everyone I have ever had sex with really."—female, 28, dating seriously for 1 year, no kids

"I wasn't supposed to tell her that her father isn't her biological father. I couldn't keep it from her anymore. I told her and now EVERYONE is mad at me, even her. I'd like to believe in honesty. Now I don't know."—male, 27, in a 2-year relationship, no kids

"My age and place of birth and my family."—female, 45, married 6 years, no kids

"How much I need more emotional and physical contact."—male, 67, married 32 years, no kids

"I never finished college."—female, 34, divorced, dating seriously for 1 year, with kids

"My financial net worth."—female, divorced, dating seriously for 1 year, with kids

"I really like her friend."—male, 26, dating seriously for 1 year, no kids

"I had a vasectomy, and my wife doesn't know."—male, 40, married 2 years, no kids

New Normal Advice

Kevin and Jenna appeared to have a normal marriage. They had two kids and a beautiful home, and both had well-paying jobs. They appeared happy, but a seemingly trivial dispute kept gnawing at the edges of their relationship. For years, Kevin had stepped into the shower every day to find Jenna's long, dark hair all over the walls. Morning after morning, year after year, he'd cleaned it up, and he told Jenna repeatedly that her hair in the shower bugged him. He also asked her to clean up after herself, but Jenna thought he was making a big deal over nothing and ignored him. Result? Kevin left for work every day angry because it really did bother him; and what bothered him more was that Jenna had so little respect for him, she wouldn't even listen to his request.

Here's how the "shower effect" can destroy a marriage. Because it was never resolved, Kevin's annoyance with Jenna was still simmering at the end of the day when he came home from work, so he'd go straight to his home office. Jenna, who had no idea he was annoyed, would call out for him to say hello to the kids while she made dinner. Kevin ignored her, telling himself he was tired and deserved a few minutes alone. Jenna would call to him again, irritated now, and again Kevin ignored her. Why should he do her bidding when she wouldn't even pay him the common courtesy of leaving the shower clean for him?

This was Jenna and Kevin's normal pattern, one they'd created together over the years without realizing it. As the shower effect grew from a ripple to a wave, it spilled over to other areas of their life, leaving them generally annoyed and disappointed in each other. The built-up resentment blunted their affection for each other and dampened their sex life and family communication. Both of them envied other couples whose interactions were relaxed and respectful, but they didn't know how to change, so this spiral of diminishing satisfaction set a dangerous new norm for their relationship.

One problem was that Jenna and Kevin each thought they knew what the other needed to be happy, but they'd never actually asked. They never talked about each other's personal priorities in life, nor had they ever discussed the things each most needed *from* the other. The solution for Kevin and Jenna was our tool "High Five!"

Since this tool works best in a relaxed setting without a lot of distractions, Jenna arranged a sitter for the children and invited Kevin out to dinner. When they were alone, she asked him to think about the top five things he needed to be happy in life, *not* including the kids or her. Kevin welcomed this question and gave it enthusiastic thought. He listed his top five passions as surfing, yoga, camping, backpacking, and biking. If he could fill his life with these activities, he'd be a happy man. Jenna listened, then shared her top five, which included networking with friends and colleagues, writing, running, travel, and enjoying the outdoors.

Why is it important to bring these lists out in the open? Because there's no negotiating your partner's happiness. Jenna couldn't argue with or deny what made Kevin happy, and vice versa. They both needed to acknowledge and respect each other's individual passions and take them into account when changing the terms of the relationship. This first step of the exercise, then, is crucial to the creation of a new normal that will satisfy both partners.

Next, Jenna and Kevin individually had to prioritize the top five changes they needed *from each other* in order to be happy. When they had completed their lists, Kevin went first, telling Jenna his number-one request: "I really need you to clean the hair out of the shower when you're done."

Jenna could not believe he'd seriously place this request in his top five, much less make it number one. Because his need didn't feel important to *her*, she was tempted to dismiss it yet again; but the rules of High Five! stopped her. As Kevin spoke, Jenna had to sit quietly and listen, processing what he was telling her without interrupting or judging him. As he talked she heard that he really was serious about this—serious enough to rank his need for her consideration as number one.

The next step is important. After Kevin finished describing his first request and before he was allowed to move on to his second need from Jenna, he had to hear her number-one request for him, which was for Kevin to spend at least ten minutes talking with the kids about their day as soon as he came home from work. Kevin was as surprised to hear that this was his wife's priority as she was to realize that his was the messy shower. He just didn't think his need for a quiet period should be that big an issue.

Now that they'd shared their top priorities with each other, they made a deal: If Jenna would clean the hair out of the shower each day, Kevin would greet the children as soon as he came home from work. This agreement took criticism out of the equation. Through give-and-take, both won.

There's a trick to making this tool work, which Kevin and Jenna discovered when they moved on to their number-two requests. The trick is to listen with an open mind and beware of defensive reactions in your partner and in yourself. If you don't, those defensive reactions can derail the benefits as they nearly did when Kevin phrased his second item for Jenna as a complaint, saying he felt like he took a backseat to her real estate job because she was always on the phone, texting, or attending networking events. Jenna's hackles went up immediately. She didn't feel like she was "always" working, and she became testy, reminding Kevin that her income helped to support the family, too. As effective as High Five! can be, it won't work if partners react this way.

Jenna's defensiveness arose out of the fear that Kevin wanted to deny her personal need for social contact beyond the family, but she needed to set this fear aside, suspend her assumptions, and try to hear what Kevin was really saying about the impact her work habits had on him. When she did this, Jenna understood that Kevin was just asking for more attention. But when she took her turn, she said the second thing that she needed from him was "to stop guilt-tripping me when I'm on the phone or networking." She explained that she felt like he was too controlling. Of course, he had a lot to say about that, but for now, he just listened.

When both of their second requests had been clearly heard, negotiations began. This might seem impossible, given the feelings of resentment and neglect involved, but the process of compromise turned out to be quite simple. Jenna offered to make an honest effort to give Kevin more attention if he, in return, would give her the emotional space to meet the demands of her job. That worked for Kevin! And now Jenna was motivated to set some boundaries and better balance her devotion to work, Kevin, and her family.

Jenna and Kevin talked further about what he specifically needed from her in order to feel prioritized and loved. They agreed she'd take time out each day to connect with him, and also set a day or two aside every so often to spend time together, just the two of them. She agreed to turn her phone off during those times. If she had a networking event one or two days in a row, she'd spend quality time with Kevin on the third day.

In the same fashion, they worked through the other requests on their lists. End result? Kevin was happy with this new normal and stopped fighting Jenna's work life, and Jenna no longer felt pushed and controlled. They both stuck to this plan, and over time it led to a new and happier normal!

Because this is one of our most valuable communication tools for couples, let's recap the High Five! rules:

GET READY: Settle down together in a quiet, comfortable room where you won't be disturbed. Each person agrees to listen with full attention and to not interrupt.

STEP ONE: Both partners think of the top five passions, activities, or interests that they individually need in their life to be happy. Important note: These choices *should not include their partner or the children*. Share the lists with each other and talk about them. Step One is nonnegiotable. You can't negiotiate what makes an individual happy. Step One is learning, understanding, and respecting what your partner needs to be happy.

Step Two: Both next take a moment to write down and prioritize the top five things their *partners* could do to make them happier.

Step Three: One person describes his or her number-one request. The other person just listens.

Step Four: *Without responding to the request just expressed,* the other person describes his or her number-one request.

Step Five: Without criticizing each other's requests, both partners negotiate a deal through trading or compromise that will allow them to honor and meet each other's requests.

Step Six: Repeat Steps Three through Five for each of the other four requests on their lists.

Sound easy? It is! And it's also surprisingly effective, as long as you speak and listen respectfully, negotiate honestly, and make a genuine effort to reach and honor a mutual agreement.

After you've moved through both partners' top five needs, it can be helpful to talk as well about what you *thought* would be on each other's list. For example, Jenna thought that Kevin's top need from her would be a hot dinner every night. Because she assumed the evening meal was important to him, she normally rushed home, no matter how busy she was, to cook for him and the family. But it turned out Kevin didn't care about dinner; he'd much rather come home to a wife who was happy to see him than to a hot meal she felt obligated to prepare. They laughed about this misunderstanding, but they were also surprised that it had led to such long-standing and needlessly negative norms in their relationship.

TOOL 20 ▶ The High Five! Fear Fighters

The High Five! tool has the power to dramatically change the quality of your communication and can bring harmony even to troubled couples. However, it can also expose deal breakers that partners are unable or unwilling to negotiate, in which case this exercise might play a role in the decision to dissolve a relationship. For this very reason, some people are reluctant to try High Five! They worry that their partners won't compromise with them on the most important issues, or that their partners will bring up an issue that they really don't want to discuss. Avoiding communication can seem like the safe way out.

If you're afraid to try the High Five! tool for any of the following reasons, fight your fear and use these suggestions:

1. <u>Are you afraid because you're overanalyzing the outcome?</u> Don't worry about *what-if* scenarios. Don't anticipate the negative or present it as a test. Instead, use this tool when you are both relaxed and communicating well. Have fun with it!

2. <u>Are you afraid because you think you already know what your partner wants from you?</u> Consider making the change right now that you expect to be number one on your partner's list, and then, after a month has passed, actually try High Five! For example, if you work late every night and you know this drives your partner crazy, do an end run around the confrontation by preemptively changing your schedule. Tell your partner that you need to work a specific number of nights, but also negotiate some good

nights for your relationship. Keep in mind, however, that it's better to use the High Five! tool sooner rather than later. You may not know your partner's wishes as well as you think.

3. <u>Are you afraid to use this tool because you're not sure what the outcome will be?</u> Rest assured that High Five! gives you your best shot at creating a new normal that will truly please you both. If you never know each other's true preferences, you'll never know what your relationship could be like. You could be really missing out.

Tool 21 ▶ Stop the Madness

The only way to stop the madness is to break the negative cycle that's been allowed to seem normal. **Stop reinforcing negative behavior.** But what if you're already way down at the bottom of the spiral? If communication has become excruciating and counterproductive, then you need a third party to help you work through this.

If you haven't already done so, find a good relationship counselor or marriage therapist. Don't delay! Nobody wants to live with a normal that's joyless, hurtful, and depressing, especially when a new and better normal is within relatively easy reach.

This is your life, so it's up to you to change it; but you shouldn't have to continuously come up with defensive mechanisms to get "the madness" to stop. If your partner isn't supporting change, then read Chapter 15 very closely to decide whether you should stay or leave this relationship.

Tool 22 ▶ Listen and Don't Speak

The easiest communication tool is to listen to what your partner says. This may sound simple, but listening well requires focus and openness. One of the main complaints of both men and women is that they never have their partner's undivided attention. If the other person isn't listening, how can you tell if you've been heard? One corrective model is the Imago therapeutic method, which includes, among other tools, an exercise in which one person speaks his or her mind, and the other partner listens until the first person stops. Then the listener recaps what he or she has heard. This is either ratified or corrected by the speaker. Once both partners agree the message has been correctly heard (it doesn't have to be agreed with, just heard), the listener gets to speak. This goes back and forth, giving each person a chance to speak and listen well. It slows down conversation and ramps up communication.

Tool 23 ▶ Don't Just Think It—Say It

Here's another simple communication tip: When you think about something positive, don't overanalyze it or hold back. Instead, share it with your partner. If you think he or she just said something smart or touching, say so! Sharing your thoughts with each other will almost always promote a better emotional connection. And it can be fun. For example, one of our couples made this tool into a game: No matter where they are or what they are doing, if one is thinking the other looks sexy or nice, they immediately say it. As a result they've shared lots of intimate thoughts with each other that they would never have shared before.

Tool 24 ▶ Our Inviolable Talk Time

Make a daily date to really talk. Any time of day will do. If you both wake up early, talk in bed or over coffee. If you can unwind together alone after work or after dinner, make that your ritual. The point is to reserve time each day to share your thoughts, experiences, and intimate feelings.

Tool 25 ▶ Time-Out

Your mother may have told you to "never go to bed mad," but, when it comes to your relationship, that's not always the best advice. It's often more constructive to let your feelings cool down before you talk than to address the problem right away, while you're still furious.

So when things get hot, take a time-out from each other. Make an appointment to talk the next day, and don't speak until then. After this break, you'll be less likely to yell at each other or be defensive or cutting.

CHAPTER 7

The Look of Love

"What?"

I f you think your partner loves you just the way you are, you're probably right; but if you think your physical image doesn't affect your relationship, think again. Overall, 88% of women and 75% of men said they believe their appearance directly affects their daily happiness and productivity. Naturally, their relationships are affected as well—more than you might imagine!

Americans, in particular, are so obsessed with their appearance that it causes them extraordinary stress. They're critical of their own bodies, faces, waistlines, skin, and hair. However, many of those who feel terrible about their looks do little or nothing physically to change. This does not escape their partner's notice.

Unfortunately, this state of affairs tends to worsen over time.

In the beginning

When a relationship is new, most of us put a lot of effort into looking our best. We somehow find the discipline to exercise, dress well, eat right, and keep our energy high. We try to look attractive. Among couples who've been together for one year or less, only 13% said they wish their partners would put more effort into their looks. Then, slowly but surely, things change. We become complacent, familiar, and the norm shifts. Instead of putting time and effort into looking great for our partner, we let other priorities take over.

The six-to-nine-year shift

From six to nine years into a relationship we see a big shift: Suddenly 43% report that their partners aren't taking care of themselves! The complaint isn't only that partners need to smarten up when they go out together, but also that they could try to look better for each other around the house.

To our surprise, we found no difference between couples with kids and those without kids when it came to attitudes about appearance. Both are just as likely, after a few years, to let looks drop down the priority list until the slackening of personal upkeep becomes an issue in the relationship. More than a third of our respondents (36%) stated that they wish their partners would make more of an effort to impress them. People who feel this way also were more likely to describe themselves as unhappy in their relationships. So why do we stop caring about how we look to our partners?

"I don't get it . . . my wife goes out of her way to look good when she goes to the gym or out to lunch with her girlfriends, then does nothing to impress me anymore."—male, 51, married 19 years, with kids

Pull it together, ladies!

We shared these data with one twenty-four-year-old who was in her second year of a serious long-distance relationship with a man who lived in another city. She felt they were so comfortable together she didn't have to worry about dressing up for him. If she picked him up at the airport in her sweats, without makeup, it was no big deal. She figured he didn't care. But she'd never bothered to ask him. After she told him about the Normal Bar results on this issue, his response surprised her. He said that her showing up in sweats made him feel as if she didn't care enough even to take two minutes to look nice for him. In fact, it was a very big deal to him! Immediately she adjusted her normal to spruce herself up to reflect how much she really did care.

Many people have the notion that a committed relationship gives them a free pass to stop worrying about their looks; but that can be a risky assumption. Some people, consciously or unconsciously, put love to the test by gaining weight, bathing infrequently, or wearing ratty old sweats and dirty jeans—even on date nights. In effect, they're daring their partners to prove they still love them. They may even treat it as a betrayal if the partner objects. This is *not* a good normal or a healthy relationship dynamic.

Most women do try to impress their partners at least some of the time. The vast majority of men (88%) who are very happy in their relationships said their partners make an effort to keep themselves up.

Only 8% of American women said they never bother; and 59% told us they make a special effort occasionally. A full third said they actually try to look great for their partners *all* the time.

Making an effort for one's partner, of course, is not just an American issue. Internationally, 8% to 26% of women won't do an extra thing to impress their lovers. To our surprise, the largest group of laissez-faire respondents were French women. Just over a quarter of *les femmes françaises* said they couldn't be bothered. Perhaps what they do for themselves is already so chic that they don't have to work any harder! However, another 74% of French women do make an effort to impress their partners at least some of the time.

> ⊕ INTERNATIONAL CHECKPOINT
>
> Who says he or she never tries to impress a partner?
>
> 26% of women in **France** say they don't try to impress their partners at all.
>
> 30% of men in **South Asia** say they never make an effort to impress their partners.

Pull it together, guys!

Appearance, of course, is an equal opportunity concern. While we think of men as needing greater visual stimulation and enjoying having a partner that other men admire, women also like their mates to look good. No woman really wants to see her man in the same shirt every day for years! And 30% of women who are very unhappy in their relationships told us their disappointment extends to their partner not taking the time to look better when going out casually and around the house.

Weighing in on Sex and Happiness

One very fit woman confided that she wanted suggestions to motivate her husband to lose weight. He'd developed a "beer belly" and, while she still loved him, she no longer found him sexy. Her ability to be aroused by her mate had waned over time—and now was completely gone. The husband was defensive and angry when approached about the issue. Neither partner was happy with the situation, but neither knew what to do. Unfortunately, this isn't an unusual situation.

When asked if they liked their partner's current weight, 40% of both men and women said no. When asked if they'd mind their partners gaining weight, 54% of men said they would mind, and 42% of women agreed.

But when the question turned to themselves, the answers became

"These jeans must have shrunk in the washer."

even more critical. More than 68% of all respondents said they'd like to lose some weight. Even assuming that some of these people did not actually need to lose weight, the high rate of self-dissatisfaction bodes poorly for these people's sex lives and relationships. When we don't like the way we look or feel comfortable with our clothes off, our self-confidence and self-esteem suffer, and it's difficult to feel sexy or worthy of sexual ardor. How can anyone who can't stand to look in a mirror bear to be seen naked, much less in passionate, uninhibited positions?

The correlation between excess weight and sexual dissatisfaction is striking. Of people who are unhappy in their sex lives, 83% said they feel they're too heavy. No wonder diet books are constantly on the best-seller lists! If only weight loss weren't so difficult for most people—and weight maintenance more difficult still.

⊕ INTERNATIONAL CHECKPOINT

Men and women who think *they* are overweight:

United States	68%
England	63%
Philippines	61%
Canada	56%
South Asia	52%
Australia	46%
Latin America	42%

People who think *their partners* are overweight:

England	43%
United States	41%
Canada	37%
Australia	33%
Spain	23%

We do see some bright spots around the world, however. We particularly admire Latin Americans and Australians, more than half of whom seem to feel better about both their own and their partners' bodies than most other populations do.

Does weight gain jeopardize the relationship?

Yes! Sixty percent of people who said they're unhappy with their overall relationships also described their partners as overweight. Being overweight complicates our lives in many ways, and relationships are not exempt.

A lot has been written on the health dangers that affect the increasingly high percentage of Americans who are overweight or obese. Being overweight is also correlated with low libido and low sexual happiness, which may help to explain why 83% of couples who are very overweight told us they're unhappy sexually. Being overweight doesn't always affect the relationship's overall happiness or commitment, but there is no doubt that when men or women are sexually dissatisfied or unhappy with a partner's appearance, it has an adverse impact on the couple's intimacy.

Looking Good Enough!

How we see and groom ourselves is one issue. How our partners see us and would like us to groom ourselves is another. But neither of these views occurs in a vacuum. We are surrounded by others to whom we are constantly comparing ourselves and each other. These comparisons can complicate—and sometimes distort—what we consider to be normal.

Americans, in particular, live in a culture that's teeming with images of models, athletes, and Hollywood celebrities who represent the height of fitness and beauty. These paragons of physical appeal are held out as examples to live up to, and many of us can't help but compare ourselves—and our partners—to them. Even though we know they're *not* representative of normal bodies and likely would be impossible for us to replicate through natural methods (even if we spent 24/7 at the gym!), there is a thriving industry that's ready and willing to "help" us *unnaturally* change our looks.

Plastic surgery
Plastic surgery is expensive and, like all surgery, medically risky. Recovery can be painful; and results vary from deeply gratifying to

deeply disappointing. Even so, we found that 4% of men and 10% of women have used cosmetic surgery to try to boost self-image. As for the others, we wanted to explore their reasons for not getting plastic surgery. Did they not believe in it? Or did the expense and surgical considerations stop them from getting "work" done?

We asked, "If you had unlimited money, would you take shortcuts to look better, such as plastic surgery, liposuction, face-lift, hair extensions, dental procedures, etc.?" In America, a shocking 65% of women and 43% of men said, yes, they would get some form of plastic surgery if only they could afford it. And about half of our respondents around the world agreed! At this rate, if the price of plastic surgery in the United States and around the world ever

⊕ INTERNATIONAL
   CHECKPOINT

Men and women who would get some form of plastic surgery if they had **unlimited** money:

Latin America	63%
United States	60%
Philippines	51%
England	46%
Canada	46%

"I got a little plastic surgery . . . what do you think?"

goes down (or the economy goes way up), we could all end up looking alike.

Some of this desire for plastic surgery must come either from personal self-image problems or from individuals' perceptions (or knowledge) that their partners would like their appearance to change. But how many of us know for sure what our partners would change about us if they could? Couples don't always give each other honest feedback, especially when it comes to appearance. So we decided to find out where the truth lies.

What physical trait would you want your partner to change?

The Normal Bar suggests that over a quarter of us (33% of men and 22% of women) would change our partners' weight if we could, and the next highest physical trait on the list is body tone. About 9% of both women and men would like their partners to be more fit.

We offered a long list of "body changes" to choose from, so it was interesting that the third most common complaint is an intimate body part. For 8.2% of men the target for change is their partner's breast size or shape. For 7.4% of women, their partner's penis size or shape could use some adjusting. But these selections could have more to do with the current barrage of advertisements for penis enlargement

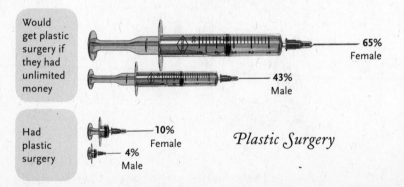

Would get plastic surgery if they had unlimited money

— 65% Female

— 43% Male

Had plastic surgery

— 10% Female

— 4% Male

Plastic Surgery

and breast augmentation than with genuine personal dissatisfaction. The power of suggestion sometimes overpowers the truth. In fact, we found no connection between penis and breast physiques and couples' happiness.

Complaint number four is teeth, at least among women. But again, this might be influenced by all the ads for teeth-whitening products now available! Men, meanwhile, are looking at the other end of the body, with about the same percentage wishing their partners had a rear end more to their liking.

The rest of the top offenders are height, signs of aging, and nose or body hair. But lest these results annoy you, rest assured that not everyone wants to change his or her partner's appearance. More than one-fourth of all our respondents told us they love the way their partners look and would not change a thing!

WISHFUL THINKING

If men and women could change one physical aspect of their partners, their top three wishes would be: 1. weight, 2. body tone, and 3. penis or breast size. But 26% would not change a thing!

It's Time to Exercise and Eat Right!

The Normal Bar clearly shows that exercising, eating well, and taking care of yourself will please your partner and improve your own daily happiness, not to mention the benefits to your health, strength, mood, and longevity. Theoretically, positive change is as close as the nearest park or fitness center. So why do so many couples who *say* they want to shape up do nothing about it?

"Don't worry, the cake is fat free and the ice cream is low fat."

Good genetics or hard work?

Fatalism is one culprit. When we asked if extremely attractive and fit physical ideals are attainable, 47% of respondents said no. That belief, that a desirable physique is impossible, is a major deterrent to working out. Not surprisingly, most people who feel this way don't bother trying to shape up at all.

We also asked, "When you see somebody who you think is perfectly fit and healthy, do you think this is due mainly to genetics, fitness, or nutrition?" An overwhelming 97.5% of men and women gave at least some credit to good genetics, and just 2.5% believe that genetics has nothing to do with it and perfect fitness and health can be entirely achieved by eating well and exercising.

Naturally, if you believe optimal fitness is only for the genetically privileged, it will seem like an exercise in futility to reach for those goals yourself. And yet our weight-conscious society makes it socially unacceptable to give up on shaping up. That leads us to invent a million excuses for not having the time, money, energy, or focus to eat better and exercise. It also makes weight a very depressing topic that fills a great many people with feelings of shame.

Sixty percent of all our couples, regardless of age or whether or not they have kids, said they rarely or never exercise together. The main reason people said they didn't encourage each other this way was lack of time, but we think other forces are at work here. If more couples exercised together, that would address several different relationship areas that our data show need work. One of the most important ones is spending time together. Ironically, couples say they don't exercise together or spend time together because they are so busy, yet when we asked the same couples how much time they spend on the computer for fun, 80% said they typically spend more than an hour every day surfing the Internet or engaging in e-chats that have nothing to do with work. Twenty-six percent answered that they spend more than three hours a day on the Internet! Clearly, there's time to be had for exercise. It's all a matter of choice.

New Normal Advice

When Natasha and Daryl were married, they were stunning. Natasha looked like a fashion model in her wedding dress, and Daryl still had the physique of the jock he'd been all through college. After work and kids began driving their lives, however, fitness and proper nutrition took a backseat. They rarely even took a walk anymore, and fresh seafood and salads were replaced by meals built around food the children preferred, such as chicken nuggets and quesadillas. A few hundred bowls of macaroni and cheese later, Natasha and Daryl each had put on ten to fifteen pounds!

One weekend, Daryl dropped in on a neighborhood basketball game and found he could barely run up and down the court. Trying to catch his breath, he thought, "What happened to me?" It wasn't just his weight and appearance that had changed; his basic physical fitness was slipping. Daryl knew he had to reverse course.

He joined a gym and started working with a trainer, who told Daryl his diet needed an overhaul. As a bonus, if he brought healthier food into the house he could bring healthier choices into his children's diet, as well. But he had to be careful how he managed this change. If he told Natasha to make more nutritious meals, she might take this as criticism and react defensively. Leading by example was the safer route, so Daryl began shopping for fresh produce himself. He volunteered to share in the cooking and started preparing healthier, lighter meals. Natasha was impressed and grateful for the help in the kitchen, and the whole family benefited.

Daryl also rearranged his schedule to make sure he exercised a couple times a week. It didn't take long before he started to look and feel better. Natasha took notice and decided to step it up a notch herself. Daryl helped her carve out time so she could exercise, too. By supporting each other, they raised the norm for the whole family.

It's important that Natasha and Daryl each made their own decision to change. We all know you can't *make* somebody else exercise or eat better, any more than you can force a friend to stop smoking. Criticizing your partner's weight or pot belly and demanding that he or she join a gym will earn you no positive results and could throw a major wedge into the relationship. If you want to encourage your partner to eat healthier and exercise, you need to *lead by example* as Daryl did. Here are some additional tools that may help.

TOOL 26 ▶ You Got Challenged—to Better Health

Take turns giving each other health challenges. Make a game of it using prizes. For example, maybe you both are going out a little too much, enjoying one too many beers or more wine than is good for you. Challenge each other to give up alcohol for three weeks. The first one that has a sip has to give the other person a back rub or foot massage. You can do this by cutting out sugar, processed foods, soda, anything unhealthy. If you both succeed in the challenge, treat yourselves to a special night out or getaway weekend. The rewards are endless!

TOOL 27 ▶ You Got Challenged—to Better Fitness

According to our data, if people would spend a little less time browsing the Web or watching TV, they could spend that time with their partners exercising. Using the You Got Challenged concept, challenge your partner to an exercise program. Even a twenty-minute walk three times a week is a great start. Make exercising together a part of your new normal way of spending time together and taking care of your bodies.

You could also do a six-week challenge program together. Each person gets to choose three fitness activities; then alternate the choices, so you try a different activity each week. Mix it up with cross training, rock climbing, martial arts, dancing, Pilates, or yoga. After six weeks, we bet you'll find something you both like to do a lot. And your relationship will benefit in multiple ways!

Tool 28 ▶ Fashion Show for Two

Go together to one of your favorite malls, department stores, or a good consignment or thrift shop and spend a few hours picking out clothes. Take turns showing each other clothes you like on yourself, then let your partner pick out clothes he or she would like to see on you. Try to leave with at least one outfit you picked out for each other, then wear your new outfit out on a date that night or later that week.

Tool 29 ▶ Two-Minute Spice

What happens when you take two minutes to tidy yourself up a little? A lot! It not only shows your partner that you care, but you'll feel better, too. Grungy clothes may be comfortable, but hanging out all day in your sweats unshowered and unclean is not likely to make you feel attractive or sexy. Take a few seconds to throw on something a little more flattering. It doesn't take much to have a big impact on your partner's reaction. And this goes for men as well as for women. Pick up any magazine that has ads for men, from *Men's Health* to *YM* to *Esquire*, and you can see what a difference is made by wearing a great suit, or a clean shirt and well-fitting jeans. Some people pride themselves on ignoring the constant drumbeat of commercialism, but to blot out all fashion and grooming cues is to ignore some useful tips. Even a small thing like aftershave lotion can perk up a partner's reception.

CHAPTER 8

Working 9 to 5 and Then Some

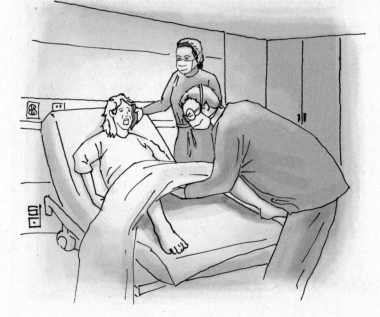

"What do you mean you can't leave the office?"

Balancing work and relationship is more of an art than a science. The relationship is central, but work, in most cases, is an economic necessity. So which comes first when they compete for the same time slot? The demands of work are often inflexible; yet if the job comes first time and time again, it can cause strains on the home front, no matter how necessary that paycheck or promotion may be.

Does your partner put his or her job first?

When we asked people if they thought their partners prioritize job over relationship, 29% of women and 28% of men answered yes. These people said they feel like an afterthought, less important than their partners' jobs. And the amount of time the partner spends at work is not necessarily the reason they feel this way. Most people who work long hours do so because their job demands it, and their partners understand this. But a little reassurance and affection at the end of the day can make up for a lot of that time—unless, of course, the extra work is *not* really required and the partner actually *does* value the job more than the relationship.

Do you and your partner enjoy your work?

When we asked if people like their own work, 61% of men and 60% of women said they find their jobs rewarding. We also asked if their partners like their jobs, and 75% of men and 67% of women said yes. We also found that those who are happy at work are much more likely to be in a happy relationship.

But what about the people who aren't so happy in their line of work?

Among those five years or less into a relationship, 22% said that unhappiness in their career adds quite a bit of tension to the relationship. Alarmingly, at ten years, this number more than doubles. More than half, or 52%, of the longer-term couples told us that their problems at work cause problems at home.

The reason couples feel more strain on their relationships after the ten-year mark may have to do with accumulated economic pressure and the stress of *needing* to work at an unrewarding job. A whopping 79% of the people who are unhappy in their work said the job was all they could find, and they had to take it to support their family.

Did your partner's career path change over the course of the relationship?

Nearly two-thirds (62%) of both men and women have made significant career changes over the course of their relationships. This includes taking on a whole new job, taking on a different position within the company, and starting their own business. Of those career changes, 68% said the switch either had no impact or positively impacted the relationship. Changing jobs seems to be a good move for most people.

Does your partner support your personal growth?

We were stunned to learn that 89% of the men and women in our study feel their partners support their personal growth. It seems there's been a worldwide change in the meaning of love and relationship! The old-school relationship model cast mating primarily as a way to produce and raise a family, but the fact that so many people in so many different countries want to support their partners' emotional, spiritual, and psychological development means that a large part of the world has embraced a new definition of coupling—one that values intimacy and deep connection.

Having your partner's support for inner change is critical. For instance, if you're in a job that you can't stand, you need to be able to talk with your mate about other options and dreams. This mutual support fosters deeper communication and will bring you closer together.

INTERNATIONAL CHECKPOINT

Do you support your partner's personal growth?

THE NORMAL BAR FOR MEN AND WOMEN

Spain	90%
USA	89%
Canada	89%
Philippines	89%
China	88%
Hungary	88%
South Asia	87%
Latin America	86%
England	85%
Scandinavia	85%
Italy	84%
France	84%

Daily Life

Not all the signals of a good relationship involve the big choices in life. Mutual support can also be measured in the ways partners help each other through the daily routine. Maybe cooking and doing the dishes together isn't glamorous, but such shared activities can make a big difference in your level of enjoyment . . . and stress. This is particularly true when both partners work outside the home.

Who normally does most of the daily chores?
We found that 42% of men and women share the daily household chores equally with their partners. However, 14% of men and 44% of

"If you're out fulfilling your lifelong dream . . .
who's going to take care of this?"

women said they do the majority of chores, so women still shoulder the lioness's share of work in the home.

The importance of this is revealed by the correlation of chore sharing and relationship happiness. Nearly half (48%) of couples who are extremely happy share housework equally, compared to just one-third (33%) of those who aren't so happy.

Who does most of the cooking?

Food preparation used to be "women's work," and women still do 50% of the cooking at home. But if we add men who are the primary chefs to those who share the cooking with their partners, we can see a big change happening in the kitchen. More than one-fourth (27%) of men do most of the cooking, and now a third of couples share kitchen chores equally.

Women
50%

Men
27%

Who's Cooking?

Men and women equally share cooking duty
23%

The domestic picture of today's relationships is clearly changing. However, it's not changing fast enough for many of our respondents. Some of their persistent complaints about inequity in daily life:

"Generally speaking, I think it's unfair that I am charged with remembering EVERYTHING—I really feel as though if I weren't

around, the kids would starve and be mute."—female, 41, married 19 years, with kids

"On a daily basis she is somewhat of a slob, but every now and then (every two weeks or so), she decides it is time for everyone to clean—even though a large part of the mess may be hers."—male, 32, married 12 years, with kids

"I end up having to be the organizer of all things, from what we're having for dinner to who's picking up the kids. Sometimes I get tired of being the grown-up all the time."—female, 32, married 10 years, with kids

"I work, she stays home. When I am home, it is usually my responsibility to watch the kids. I never get a break."—male, 36, married 6 years, with kids

"We live in a traditional Indian joint family with our parents. This means ladies do all the housework even though I do go out to work and earn money. I find this really unfair."—female, 28, married 4 years, no kids

"Even though I work full-time outside the home, and my husband stays home to work on his Internet business, he doesn't consider housework to be something that he needs to do."—female, 36, married 12 years, with kids

"I work and she goes to school, but she also does a lot of cooking and cleaning. I might help but she enjoys cooking and I just don't *care to have the house as clean as she wants it."* —male, 27, in a 2-year domestic partnership, no kids

"I don't think I should do all the laundry." —female, 40, divorced, in a 1-year domestic partnership, with kids

"Chores aren't done unless I prompt it. I feel like a nag and he is much messier than me." — female, 33, married 7 years, no kids

New Normal Advice

Quentin and Meagan exemplifed the kind of hard-driving professionals whose marriage suffers because they put their careers ahead of each other. Both were under a lot of pressure. Quentin's law firm had made it clear that he was not being "productive" enough, and Meagan was working full-time as a sales rep while trying to get an advanced degree online. When they came home from work they were always behind on household duties, and they argued about who was supposed to do what.

Both of them felt unappreciated and unsupported. Quentin thought Meagan was so absorbed in her own troubles that she had no interest in his, and Meagan would avoid Quentin for the first half hour after he came home because he was always sullen and angry. One afternoon they had a huge fight, accusing each other of letting the car's brakes get dangerously worn, and they didn't speak for days afterward.

Quentin and Meagan needed to change their normal, and they needed to do it quick. So Meagan asked her neighbors Hannah and Kenny how they managed work and household duties. Kenny said that one of the benefits of working hard was having a little more money to spend, so he and Hannah had hired a house-cleaner. For $70 one day a week the house would get a good clean-ing. Well worth it! Then Kenny and Hannah split other household duties according to their individual preferences. Kenny didn't mind going to the grocery store but hated to cook. So Hannah did most of the cooking and Kenny did the shopping. They split the rest of the chores according to who had more time, and if one person was doing too much, then the person making more money would pay for help rather than putting the extra work on the partner. Kenny and Hannah were both happy to buy themselves out of as many chores as they could afford, so in good times they had both a cleaner and a gardener come once a week.

Meagan liked the sound of Kenny and Hannah's solution. She and Quentin couldn't afford help once a week, but after a few calcula-tions, she concluded that they could have someone come in to help twice a month. Then she and Quentin sat down to discuss who liked what chores better, and they split them accordingly. By making each task someone's stated responsibility, they avoided the problems that arose when a specific job was unassigned. Their new normal gave them each a clearer stake in running the household, and it also gave them each more support, which made them both happier.

Much of the anxiety that accompanies the juggling of work and housework can be resolved through negotiation. Most of us don't con-trol our jobs, the hours we work, or the pay we get, but there's often room for more flexibility and communication on the home front. It's important to let your partner know what's bothering you (such as having to make dinner after returning home from a long day at the office, or coming home to a dirty and disorganized house), and to offer suggestions for change.

Here are some other tools to help you make the sorts of simple but necessary corrections that can radically improve the daily quality of your relationship.

Tool 30 ▶ Let's Make a Deal

If you want your partner to do something but don't want to sound like you're complaining or criticizing, offer to make a deal. Let's say you're sick and tired of doing all the cooking and cleaning. Instead of making a fuss about it, think of a trade that you can offer for your partner's help. Then wait for a relaxed opportunity to tell your partner that you want to make a deal. For example, say, "Honey, I'll do all the grocery shopping (even if you already do) and rub your shoulders after dinner if you'll help cook or take care of all cleanup." Make an offer so exciting, fun, or pleasurable that your partner can't refuse. You'll not only accomplish your goal, but you'll do it without argument.

Tool 31 ▶ Weekly Team Conference

Each week, gather your family together and take inventory of what isn't working, and what is. Give kudos for last week's improvements and identify targets for this week. Organize a team approach to a big problem (perhaps dirty bathrooms or a garage that no one can even get into anymore). Make a plan for Tuesday and Thursday to be "cook your own dinner" nights (even if that dinner is an omelet or heating up last night's leftovers). Brainstorm problem areas to come up with innovative solutions, such as cooking together to produce a big pot of soup or an extra casserole on Sunday that can be frozen so you have several ready-made dinners throughout the week. The point is to involve everyone in the process.

Tool 32 ▶ Job Happy Talk

We all have a tendency to complain about the stuff that bothers us. But hearing only bad news usually creates an aversive reaction—especially if it's the first thing that your partner hears when you walk in the door! So make a point of bringing home at least one upbeat story about work each day. It doesn't have to be anything major. Intriguing office gossip will do, or an interesting or amusing customer. Or describe something funny that happened at your child's school. Share the good stuff as well as the bad so your partner feels connected to your "other" lives.

Tool 33 ▶ Grab a Sick Day

One way to remind your partner what truly matters most is to take a day off—together. If you're entitled to a personal day, use it! If not, consider using a sick day for relationship health. No one is suggesting that you do this often, but even once would show your partner how much you value your time together, even with all the other demands on your time and attention.

Tool 34 ▶ Be a Change Agent at Work

Sometimes employers forget that workers have families, relationships, and a need for some flexibility. But if you ask or petition someone at the top who understands the value of happy employees, you might discover that there's some wiggle room. For example, if you offered to work some of your hours at night you might be able to gain some free daytime. If you could arrange to work at home one day a week, you might get certain work done more efficiently and also be able to have lunch with your partner. Small changes that are insignificant to your boss can be a boon to your relationship.

CHAPTER 9

Dollars and Sense

"Who needs a bunch of money when you have me?"

Remember how often as a kid you were asked, "If you could have one wish, what would it be?" Then, before you could answer, the person asking would quickly add, "You can't say all the money in the world!" Money's too obvious, because *everybody*, it seems, wants more of it.

Our survey asked a variation on this question, followed by choices:

If you could be guaranteed any of the following right now, which would you choose?

    1. To be incredibly fit

2. To be very good-looking

3. To have unlimited money

4. To have an amazing body

5. To be in perfect health

6. To be extremely intelligent

The Normal Bar shows that 45% of all people want unlimited money. The results were the same for those who are extremely happy in their relationships as for those who are in absolutely miserable relationships. Surprisingly, even having "perfect health" took a backseat to money; only 32% of men and women chose health first. No matter what else is going on in their lives, it seems, people would rather be rich than anything else. But is it wise to prize money so highly?

⊕ INTERNATIONAL
    CHECKPOINT

Men and women in Canada said they'd rather have good health than more money.

Does money buy happiness?

We found that having more money does *not* make for a happier relationship. Asked to rate themselves on a scale of one to nine, one being extremely *unhappy* and nine being extremely *happy* as a couple, about 72% of respondents registered in the upper scale of happiness—with almost *no* correlation to financial income. If anything, the richest couples in our study were marginally less likely to be happy.

Money may not be the golden ticket to a happier relationship, but it does have a number of negative and positive side effects that are worth mentioning. For example, the *belief* that money produces happiness can undermine couples if one partner wishes the other earned more—especially if the dissatisfied partner actively begins looking for a richer alternative. In cases like this, the relationship might already be shaky, as money is rarely the only issue. Nevertheless, a belief that more money is a path to happiness can further weaken a fragile relationship.

I want to be with somebody with more money!

When we asked, "Do you wish you were in a committed relationship with someone who makes more money than your partner does?" 35% of women and 23% of men said yes. That is a substantial number of people who feel that their present partner doesn't meet their financial ambitions or needs.

But wait! The Normal Bar shows that money has no impact on happiness, so why do all these people want a richer partner? One reason may be that perception is more powerful than reality. The belief that money can buy happiness is so firmly entrenched in our society that, for many people, it takes more than facts to shake it.

Another reason may be that some of these couples are truly strapped—and strained—for cash. Not having enough money to pay bills, afford medical care, or meet other basic needs can drain the joy out of daily life and cause friction within relationships. A replacement partner with the ability to solve the family debt crisis could seem pretty attractive under these circumstances! With high unemployment rates, volatile stock pension funds, and a shaky housing market, it's not surprising that money is one of the top three sources of stress in relationships.

Financial worries

Fifty percent of men and women worry about money, and these worries tend to escalate the stress on relationships as income drops. Among couples with an income of $20,001 to $37,750, more than 62% told us that money worries affect their relationships. And 68%

Income vs. Happiness

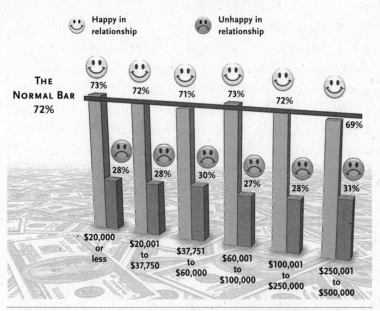

Percentages in each income category may not sum to exactly 100% due to rounding.

of men and women who are worried about money also are very dissatisfied sexually. By contrast, only 28% of higher-income people are troubled by the impact of finances on their relationships.

Financial stability is not the only concern, however. How a couple communicates about money is also pivotal. Our data show that couples need to be open with each other about spending, investing, and saving, no matter how much money they have. The more solid, cooperative, and trusting their interactions over money, the better a couple can weather financial insecurity. This may help to explain why 65% of all those who are extremely happy in their relationships told us they're *not* worried about their finances.

Money Management

Money is often a taboo topic. Most of us consider our debt, income, savings, and financial management decisions to be confidential, to be shared with our partners and few others. You might be shocked to know that one-fourth of the people in the Normal Bar study don't even talk about how much they earn with their spouse! And that percentage climbs even higher among committed but *unmarried* couples, 40% of whom never discuss details about their finances. This is a serious relationship pitfall.

Financial communication

We discovered that openness about money definitely correlates with relationship satisfaction. Among extremely happy couples, 80% of partners know how much their significant other earns. On the negative side, here are some comments that reflect the dangers of *not* being open and cooperative about money matters:

HIDDEN ASSETS?

25% of men and women do not talk with their spouse about how much they earn.

"I'm steadily looking for a job and just looked at our financial accounts, which my wife has been handling (for the bills) for the last year. I nearly had a heart attack when I saw how much money she's been spending. She's disappointed me so badly, I don't even know where to begin." —male, 42, married 8 years, with kids

"I came into the relationship knowing we would be splitting bills equally. But I would never have thought it would come down to

splitting the cost of a gallon of milk. If he goes to the store to buy anything, such as milk, he leaves me the receipt on the kitchen counter with a note that says that I owe him $1.75." —female, 52, married 2 years

"I'd like to marry my girlfriend of 3 years, but I refuse to marry her debt." —male, 27

"I have my credit card statements sent to my office." —female, 39, married 10 years

"We've tried to talk about a budget and spending, and it always turns into an argument. She feels like everything we own has to be new!" —male, 33, married 4 years

Do people who earn a lower income argue more?

You might expect that couples who struggle to make ends meet would have more heated financial arguments than well-heeled spouses, but that's not the case, according to the Normal Bar data. About 45% of all couples argue about money, but those who earn $20,000 or less actually argue *less* frequently about money than do couples who earn $250,000 to $500,000! The inconvenient truth here is that people tend to spend just a little more than they have, so people who earn $250,000 and more still have plenty to argue about. And they do.

Who argues the most? The middle class! Why? Perhaps because the middle class is caught in the

MONEY HASSLES

Couples who earn $20,000 or less argue less frequently about money than couples who earn $250,000 to $500,000.

Argue About Money

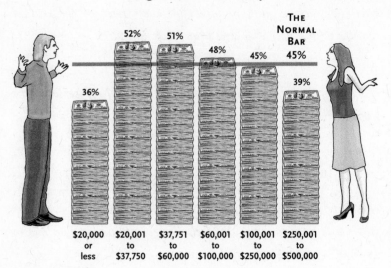

| 36% | 52% | 51% | 48% | 45% | THE NORMAL BAR 45% | 39% |

| $20,000 or less | $20,001 to $37,750 | $37,751 to $60,000 | $60,001 to $100,000 | $100,001 to $250,000 | $250,001 to $500,000 |

particularly frustrating position of earning more than the struggling working class but not enough to guarantee the comfortable lifestyle they feel entitled to. Middle-class status in America used to mean security, but in today's economy, with the high costs of housing, gas, and other formerly affordable essentials, security is out of reach for many who hold what used to be middle-class jobs. The frustration of unmet expectations can cause more friction in relationships than does the absence of funds that were never anticipated in the first place. When couples have poor money management skills, that also can add to the strain.

Separate accounts becoming more important

A surprising 60% of childless partners keep separate bank accounts, and an unexpectedly large number of partners *with* kids (40%) also hold at least some of their money separately. In fact, 36% of all couples who've been together for more than twenty years still keep separate bank accounts. This means a major change has occurred in American families.

It used to be a matter of course for couples to merge bank accounts when they married. Keeping money separate was seen as a threat or contradiction to committed marriage. Today, however, both partners are likely to have built up significant savings before marriage, and many men and women continue to keep their individual finances separate even after marriage. High divorce rates, and especially the media coverage of celebrity divorces, have highlighted the hassle it can be to divide property and money when couples break up. With this in mind, even new couples are opting for more economic independence and safety.

Time together does reduce mistrust, and convenience makes it more likely to merge money, but the Normal Bar shows that over a third of long-term couples still keep separate accounts. At least in the United States, that is looking like a new normal.

Access and control

The idea of a joint approach to money isn't gone, however. Comingling assets is still one major way of declaring and creating "coupleness." So, even though their accounts may be separate, it may be mostly symbolic since 62% of all married couples say they have equal access to and control of each other's bank funds and investments. Moreover, ATM cards, online accounts, and other changes in banking and finance have blurred the distinction between separate and joint access and control of finances. And, surprisingly, a slightly larger number of *unmarried* couples (66%) share equal access and control of all bank accounts and investments. This is romantic and efficient, but perhaps not entirely wise, since the breakup rate of cohabiting couples is about 50%.

Decision making

Does the primary breadwinner normally decide how money gets spent in the household? Not usually. We found that 77% of married couples decide jointly how money is spent. That is certainly good news for the lower-earning partners, and it indicates that most couples are trying to have an egalitarian relationship.

However, another 16% of men and women said that the partner who does the child rearing does *not* get an equal say in how money is spent. As in previous generations, there are still many women (or men) who sacrifice economic parity when they stay home with the kids. And in many countries outside America, even aspiring to an egalitarian relationship is still seen as abnormal.

> ## To Earn Is Not to Spend
>
> *In 77% of couples, the person who makes more money does* not *get more control over how the money is spent.*

Prenup

There was a time when prenuptial agreements were reserved for tycoons and superstars. They were also viewed as something of an insult to the partner who was being excluded from preexisting wealth. The idea of dividing money before exchanging vows seemed to many to violate the spirit of marriage and perhaps even doom the relationship before it began. Why, the reasoning went, would you plan to keep money separate unless you were planning an exit strategy before you were even engaged? Now that reasoning has clearly changed.

A majority (53%) of our married couples said they'd have had no problem with a prenup had their partners asked for one before tying the knot. Although only 3.6% of our American married couples

"A prenup? Seriously? You don't even have anything."

actually *have* a prenup, these agreements no longer seem to carry the negative stigma they used to.

Wills

Discussing and planning for the eventuality of a partner's death is so difficult for most couples that they can't bring themselves to do it. An alarming 61% of all couples in this study do not have a will!

What's worse, 47% of couples with children do not have a will. If something were to happen to both parents, much of these children's inheritance could be jeopardized.

Many movies have plots built around big surprises in someone's will, so we wondered if couples who do have a will have shared all

Worst-Case Scenario

47% of couples with children do not *have a will!*

the contents with each other. That answer is overwhelmingly yes. Only 1.5% of all people said there's something in their will that their partners do not know about. Most people who make the effort to draw up a will apparently do so without any secret motives.

Splitting the bill

Not so long ago, the guy always picked up the check for expenses. Now in America that norm has shifted, at least among committed couples. While dating, men still do the lion's share of paying for an evening out, but more than half of married couples split all the bills, and 23% of married duos split some of their bills. Only 25% of married couples have one partner who pays for everything. And in 8% of the couples, that one partner is female.

Is bill splitting more common in happier relationships? Not really. Half of the people who split their bills are also extremely happy with their relationships, but the other 50% are dissatisfied with their relationships. So sharing expenses isn't likely to affect your happiness as a couple.

What is the new working relationship normal? The Normal Bar data suggest that it's the couple who shares household expenses and financial decision making. In fact, the husband as total manager and decision maker may have become a myth some time ago, but now not even the myth survives.

Our data clearly show that women are contributing more financially to the household income and take a larger part in financial decision making even when they aren't currently working outside the household. Attitudes have changed markedly in response to the current economy, which typically makes it a necessity for both partners to work to make ends meet, and also in response to changing perspectives on the value of housework and child care. It's no longer a foregone conclusion that just because one partner works at home, managing the household and the kids, it means that she—or he—has less of a say in financial decisions. As a result, we are starting to see more men stay home with kids, while their wives are the primary breadwinners.

New Normal Advice

Ginny and Mario are at odds about how they handle their finances. In the "old country," Mario's father never talked about money, did not want to be questioned about it, and kept his wife on an allowance for all the household expenses. Mario's dad wasn't well off and the allowance rarely covered their bills. The couple had terrible fights about money, and Mario confided in Ginny that as a child he would hide on paydays because his dad and mom always screamed at each other. Nonetheless, after their second child was born, Mario followed his father's example.

Because Ginny's salary wouldn't cover much more than the cost of child care, they both decided she should stay home. Soon thereafter, the money fights began. Ginny didn't want to engage in screaming matches, but she felt that Mario was now making economic decisions unilaterally and she resented his snide remarks about how she spent "his" money. She felt the respect between them sliding, and she wanted reinstatement as a full partner in their relationship.

Fortunately, Mario didn't want to act like a tyrant; he agreed that they should sit down, discuss what was bothering her, and try to change the way things were going.

What they worked out was a total budget that gave *each* of them a finite amount of money. If the allotments weren't enough, they'd discuss them at each Friday night's "business meeting," where they'd review the week and discuss any changes that could make finances work better. This soon became an enjoyable part of their week and their relationship.

Then they decided to join an investment club. Working with the small amount of money they reserved for the stock market, Ginny became the family financial expert. She turned out to have a knack for it and over time earned a return at least even with those of the professionals. Mario was delighted with her and the extra income, and they both took pride in their ability to sidestep the traumatic pattern of his childhood parental battles.

TOOL 35 ▶ Money Talks

Not talking about money issues doesn't make money problems go away. It only creates more stress in the relationship. So start talking more about how you feel about your finances currently and where you would like to be economically in five, ten, and twenty years. An easy way to do this is to work toward a specific and rewarding goal. Plan a vacation you want to take together or as a family. Set a budget for the trip and work together to set money aside for the trip, all the while watching your spending and paying down debt. When you're both looking forward to a goal you set together, you'll be surprised at the communication that opens up around finances.

TOOL 36 ▶ Mad Money

It's good to have some money of your own that you don't have to negotiate about with each other, so figure out how much "mad money" you can each afford to put away. Even if you have limited means, try to save a few dollars now and then. Over time, this fund will grow, and sometimes just that little bit of private wiggle room can take the competition out of financial communication. You both need the freedom to make unilateral spending decisions every now and then.

TOOL 37 ▶ Promise You Won't Get Mad

Why don't people talk more openly about finances? Often it's because they're afraid of their partner's reaction. So one way to improve financial communication is to make an agreement with your partner: You'll talk more openly about bills, credit card debt, purchases, etc., if he or she will promise not to get mad. If you both can keep the anger out of the discussion, economic communication will become less threatening, and it will be easier to establish a new normal and get your finances under control.

CHAPTER 10

Friends and Family

"Dave told me when we first got married, his friends were
part of the package."
"Wow, you must love him very much."

Your friends have been there for you. They know about the
bad dates, the times you were dumped and hurt; and they've
been a reality check—perhaps many times—when you needed one.
You share a lot of good memories with them and, while you know
they have their flaws, they're part of your history. When you first
told them, "This is the one," they may have been thrilled for you,
or maybe they voiced caution—or outright concern. However they
reacted, you persevered and here you are, perhaps with supportive

friends who enhance your relationship, perhaps not. Either way, you want to keep those friends in your life; but it's not always easy to find, much less maintain, the balance between friends and the one you love. And remember, your partner faces the same challenge!

Do your partner's friends interfere in your relationship?

It's never fun if you feel you have to compete for your partner's attention. Fortunately, this is not a common problem. Only 16% of women and 11% of men told us that their partner's friends often disrupt the relationship. Most people think of friends as a positive element of both their personal lives and their relationships. However, if friends do become a problem, their interference can have significant negative consequences. Disruptive and interfering friends are a complaint of 23% of the people who are in unhappy relationships. For example:

"His friends never liked me. They never gave me a chance because they liked his first wife so much. So every time we have a problem, they are like this chorus of 'I told you so' or 'what a bitch.' He tells me what they say, which is part of the problem. Now I don't trust them and don't want them around, and that makes more problems."—female, 48, married 2 years, no kids

"Her friends are snobs. They make it clear that my friends are beneath them. Thanksgiving last year was a disaster. They were actually snickering at my friends' toasts. I don't want to be in a social situation with them again."—male, 42, married 4 years, no kids

"I don't like being with her friends. It's all shop talk. Fine if you are in the real estate business but really tiresome if you aren't. It's

clear to me that they don't care if I am bored or not. I find excuses to not be there or leave early. This isn't the way I want to spend our time."—male, 34, married 5 years, with kids

"*His best friend lived with us for a while and he was single. Not long after, my husband decided he wanted a divorce.*"—female, 37, married 12 years, with kids

"*My husband's ex-wife is our financial planner, and he maintains a relationship with her. This is very difficult for me.*"—female, 58, married 9 years, with kids

Are you friends with your partner's family?

If you don't like your partner's family, you're more alone than you may have thought. A large majority—80% of women and 83% of men—said they like their partner's family. This may, however, have something to do with the frequency of contact. More than half, or 55%, hardly ever see their in-laws. Another 25% see them about once a month; and just 20% see them frequently. In this case, absence really may make the heart grow fonder.

HAPPY IN-LAWS

Internationally, between 75% and 85% of men and women like *their partner's family.*

Does your partner have an old lover or spouse who's still in the picture?

Is it normal to maintain friendships with past lovers and spouses? Not according to the Normal Bar. Only 26% of women and 21% of

"Don't be silly. Of course he likes you."

men in America said their partners still keep past lovers as friends, and this finding was repeated internationally.

And yet, when former lovers *are* around, they're not necessarily a problem. When we asked these respondents if they're bothered by their partners' friendship with the ex, 68% of the men and 50% of the women said they're fine with it. Either they don't feel threatened by the ex, or the partner has children with the ex, in which case an amicable relationship among all the adults is beneficial. Or both. Having a high level of satisfaction and trust within the relationship, as well as familiarity with the partner's ex, can make a big difference.

INTERNATIONAL
CHECKPOINT

Only 19% of people in **China** said their former lovers were still a part of their lives.

How does your relationship compare to your friends'?
Does it matter?

It's only natural to compare your relationship to those of your friends. We found that 46% of all people think their relationships are happier than their friends', 37% say it's about equal, and 17% think their relationships are less happy. However, the longevity of a relationship makes a big difference in these perceptions. Just 6% of couples who've been together for a year or less—who are still in the honeymoon phase—think that their friends are happier. Ten years into the relationship, 21% think their friends are happier. This suggests that the response may say more about the person's own relationship than it does about the friends'. If you think your friends' marriages are happier than yours, consider this a sign that your own relationship needs some attention.

Have you ever intentionally misled your friends to
believe your relationship is better than it is?

Is it normal for couples to pretend they're happy? Yes! More than half, or 53%, of the people who are unhappy to slightly happy in their relationships pretend to be happy when talking to or spending time with friends. And 39% of those who are downright miserable in their relationships also hide their unhappiness.

Their reasons range from shame to hope that if they don't label the marriage as "in trouble," things might get better. Unfortunately, when things don't get better, friends often feel deliberately misled and hurt by the lack of trust and confidence that the deception indicates.

False Pretenses

It's normal for over half of men and women to pretend they are happier with their partners than they really are.

The illusion that most couples are perfectly happy is just that—an illusion. Those who are unhappy gain nothing by pretending to be ideal; and the rest of us would do well to remember that most relationships are more complex behind the scenes than they are in public!

Parenthood

To have or not to have? At some point, usually quite early in the relationship, most couples begin to talk about starting a family. Should they, or shouldn't they? If so, when should they start, and how many kids should they have? If they're smart, the couple will also discuss how they're going to integrate their love life and identity as a couple with the obligations and financial sacrifices that parenthood requires. No matter how diligently they try to anticipate the changes that children will bring, few couples are fully prepared for all the compromises that family life demands.

Do you think having kids brought you and your partner closer or pushed you further apart?

About the same number of men (43%) as women (41%) believe that their children have brought them closer to their partners. Only 16% (15% female and 18% male) said their kids pushed them further apart; and 43% (44% female and 39% male) said parenthood neither brought them closer nor pushed them apart. Other studies have chronicled the fatigue and loss of intimacy that some parents experience when their children are babies and again when the kids go through adolescence. The impact on relationship is more pronounced if the child or children have special psychological, physical, or behavioral needs. Nonetheless, children are rarely the direct cause of conflict or distance between parents.

"Hi, sweetheart! I'm sure it won't be too long before we'll be
able to sit next to each other again."

Have there been periods when the only thing holding your relationship together was your children?

Men and women gave virtually the same answer when asked if there
have been times when they would have left the relationship if not for
their kids. The Normal Bar shows that for 65% of couples, kids are
not the glue that holds them together. Another 20% said the kids
have been a binding factor on occasion, and 12% said that having
kids kept them together over a long stretch of time. Only 3% said
children are the only thing that keeps them together, period.

During times of turmoil, then, children can be an important
factor in preserving relationships. Investment in their kids kept one-
third of our couples together long enough to solve or come to terms
with whatever was causing big problems, and these couples wound up
happier as a result.

There's also good news in the fact that only 3% of couples said they're together solely because of their kids. In the past, couples with children were normally pressured to stay together no matter how miserable they were. Today the prevailing wisdom is that children are better served by a happy home, and the Normal Bar reflects this change.

When you're alone with your partner, how much time do you spend discussing the kids or parenting?

Couples seem to find a nice balance between talking about the kids and talking about each other. Nearly three-fourths, or 74%, of both men and women said that when they're together, they spend a quarter of their time or less talking about parenting or their kids. That seems like a good ratio for romance! Another 24% said they keep these discussions to half of their alone time, which still leaves a healthy amount of time for intimacy. Just 2% said that all they talk about are their kids and parenting. We don't have to ask them how romantic their lives are together!

What kind of a parent do you think your partner is?

Wouldn't you like to be called a "gifted" parent? Well, 18% of men and 7% of women feel that their partners have this gift. Another 51% of men and 42% of women score their partner's parenting as at least excellent. More kudos go to women than to men, which is understandable since more women are the primary parent, but men also get high praise.

In fact, most parents get such high ratings that the 37% of women and 24% of men who describe their partners as just "good" seem almost to be demeaning them. Still, good is likely good enough. The same can't be said for the 12% of women and 5% of men who

Report Card

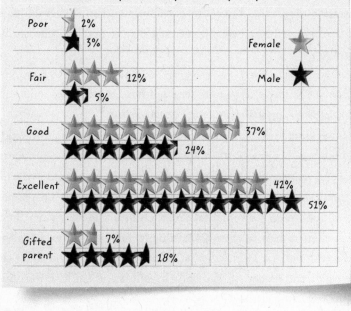

What kind of parent do you think your partner is?

	Female	Male
Poor	2%	3%
Fair	12%	5%
Good	37%	24%
Excellent	42%	51%
Gifted parent	7%	18%

Percentages for men do not sum to exactly 100% due to rounding.

labeled their partner's parenting as "fair," much less for the remaining few who consider their partner's parenting skills "poor." In these cases, for the sake of the whole family, some parenting lessons may be in order!

New Normal Advice

Matt and Desiree had been living together for more than six years when Matt decided that Desiree wasn't "the one" and broke it off. Desiree, who'd hoped to marry Matt, was devastated; however, the two remained friends. Months later, when Matt began a serious relationship with Sherry, he didn't think this new relationship should affect his friendship with Desiree. In fact, because Desiree was studying massage, she stopped by to practice giving Matt a massage one day while Sherry was at work. Although Matt assured Sherry that he no longer had any romantic feelings for Desiree, Sherry had a big problem with their friendship and with the massage. Who wouldn't?

It wasn't that Sherry didn't trust Matt. She was actually quite secure and knew that old girlfriends were not necessarily a threat to her relationship. But Sherry told Matt that afternoon massages were not OK, and she was also uncomfortable with his many lunches with Desiree. After some rather intense conversations, they came to a mutual agreement that if Matt wanted to continue being friends with Desiree, then Sherry needed to get to know her better and be invited along too. Matt agreed this was a fair request.

The next time Desiree invited Matt to lunch, Matt said he wanted to invite Sherry, too. Desiree welcomed the idea, and they all went to lunch. Sherry and Desiree hit it off so well that, some months later, when Desiree was in a relationship of her own, the two couples went out together!

When you have spent a good chunk of your life with somebody, it can be nice to keep that individual in your life. Our data show that a lot of people do and it works out just fine, but you have to keep your current partner's feelings in the forefront. That's why, when Sherry asked for boundaries to be set, Matt was wise to comply. Setting boundaries is also important for a relationship when it comes to family members and friends. And boundaries don't just apply to physical time with other people but also to time spent on the phone, e-mail, texting, or Facebook. If you're unhappy with the amount of energy your partner puts into a past relationship, friend, or family member, sit down together and set boundaries you both can accept.

TOOL 38 ▶ Not Inflicting Friends

Why not be honest about which of your partner's friends you enjoy and which you'd rather see less frequently? Your partner's old friends may be precious, but if they're not precious to you, encourage your partner to see them alone. If that would be too difficult, discuss the circumstances that would be most and least amenable to you. For example, it might be fine to invite these old friends to a party but not to go skiing or camping with them.

TOOL 39 ▶ One Is Silver and the Other Is Gold

Sometimes couples forget to make new friends together and thus miss out on a strong source of relationship strength. New friends help bring novel experiences into the relationship. They can stimulate new topics for conversation and widen your spectrum of activities. Try to cultivate different kinds of friendships. Reach beyond the workplace and the other parents at your child's school or team, so you're making friends with a wide array of interests. Friends can help you have more fun as adults so you don't think of yourselves only as Mom and Dad.

PART

III

Staying Together

CHAPTER 11

Keeping the Sexual Flame Alive

"It's all about the love. If you are happy, the love flows, the intimacy is strong. When I'm in love, and love my partner unconditionally, I'm in a love zone. I want to pleasure him in every way, and vice versa."—female, 68, married 25 years

Does sexual satisfaction change over the years? A little, but not as much as you might suspect. We found that 82% of couples start off with a deep sexual connection at year one, and six to nine years into the relationship, three-fourths of all couples who describe their relationships as happy still describe their sex lives in terms of "lovemaking," rather than as "efficient" or "warm" or "pleasant." That percentage only shrank to 67% at twenty-five years plus, and just 2%

of happy couples have sex lives that are unsatisfying. Granted, this means that about a fourth of those who are in happy relationships at the six-to-nine-year phase would rather their sex lives were more passionate or deeply emotional—but they're good candidates for change if they choose to seek help. It is also worth pointing out that those relationships in which people were least happy or least sexually satisfied are more likely to have already dissolved and are those less likely to be in the Normal Bar sample of people in relationships.

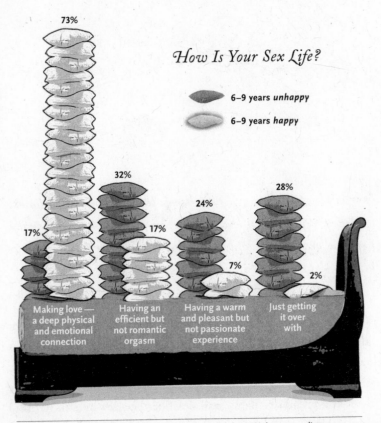

How Is Your Sex Life?

6–9 years *unhappy*

6–9 years *happy*

73%

32%

24%

28%

17%   17%

7%

2%

Making love — a deep physical and emotional connection

Having an efficient but not romantic orgasm

Having a warm and pleasant but not passionate experience

Just getting it over with

Percentages for unhappy respondents do not sum to exactly 100% due to rounding.

People in unhappy relationships, not surprisingly, are far less likely to feel good about their sex lives. However, 17% of those who say they're unhappy still *do* have a passionate and/or emotionally connected sex life.

Consider Sophia and Michael. They're first-generation Italian Americans, and their relocation from Ravenna, Italy, to Connecticut has been tough for them. Their small restaurant, which they run together, has been hit hard by a tough economy, and an additional loan they were counting on from family hasn't come through. Although young—twenty-five and twenty-seven, respectively—they have a three-year-old, and Sophia has just found out two things she wasn't ready for: First, she's pregnant again; and second, Michael has been cheating on her with her cousin.

One might imagine that a couple in this set of circumstances would fight a lot, be on the verge of a breakup, and seldom have sexual relations—much less enjoy a passionate and meaningful sex life. But while there's plenty of fighting, as well as accusations, tears, and threats, in Michael and Sophia's house, sex is not a problem. According to Sophia, in bed they're "fierce, loving, can't get enough of each other—but only in the bedroom." Their physical connection is so strong that it gets them through what can only be described as a daily soap opera. "Very Catholic" and "married for life," they expect to work things out, no matter what.

Sexual Frequency

If you're worried that everyone but you is having sex all the time, worry no more. Only about 7.5% of our sample said they have sex daily. Forty percent of all our couples said they normally have sex three to four times a week, and about a quarter of our respondents (27%) only have sex a handful of times a month, about 9% once a month. Another 17.5% of our respondents told us they have sex rarely (13%) or never (4.5%). But all these statistics rearrange when we consider how duration and quality of relationship impact sexual frequency.

Sexual frequency over the years in a relationship

The Normal Bar shows that the frequency of sex in a relationship does typically decline over the years, though not so much for the partners who said they're very happy or extremely happy with their sex lives. In their first year together 67% of these happy couples have sex three to four times a week. And after twenty-one years together, 60% of couples who are extremely happy with their sex lives *still* have sex three to four times a week. This means that age and duration are no obstacle if a couple's norm encourages and celebrates sexual connection. General happiness, high sexual frequency, and sexual happiness seem to be a package.

Sadly, when we look at the couples who said they're unhappy with their sex lives, we find that nearly 70% of them never or rarely have sex anymore. This is more common than most people realize, because couples know it is taboo not to have sex, and they're embarrassed to find themselves in a sexless marriage; thus, many choose to keep the problem secret. So if your friends say they're unhappy about their sex lives, the situation may be more dire than you think.

The sexual frequency (intercourse) magic number

Are couples who have sex frequently happier over the years than couples who don't have sex as often? Yes, they really are. Three to four times a week is the magic frequency!

You may be thinking that sex can't mean that much after twenty or thirty years of a solid relationship. A lot of people (primarily women) believe that you can have a great relationship if sex is infrequent or even absent. But quite a few other studies corroborate our findings: If you are having sex only a couple times a month or less, your relationship may be suffering (unless, of course, there is an inescapable reason such as very poor health, depression, taking medications that depress libido, or being in a commuting relationship). A minimal sex life, especially for people under seventy, generally indicates an undercurrent of problems, emotional distance, anger, or serious psychological distress on the part of one or both partners.

A drop in sexual frequency may be a symptom of other problems or conditions, but it can become a source of emotional distress itself if viewed by one or both partners as a form of rejection, punishment, or disinterest. Not everyone has the same sexual needs, and some people have never found intercourse a bonding or pleasurable aspect of life, but it's rare for both partners to feel that way; so, even if one partner doesn't mind a slowed-down or even extinguished sex life, it's likely the other partner does.

MORE SEX = HAPPY COUPLE

The happiest couples make love three to four times a week.

Yes, couples who rarely have sex can be in love, but that doesn't mean they're particularly happy. Frequency of sex, especially when a couple lives together, can indicate whether or not the relationship is in good enough shape to last.

Sexual frequency: having kids versus no kids

The rumors about sex and children are true: Raising children does tend to interfere with sexual frequency. These are two competing demands. Both are emotionally compelling, and both require quality as well as quantity time. When people want children, they generally want them passionately. And the same goes for wanting each other. Sex is a strong expression of a deep emotional connection between two people, and so is having a child. But the needs of children often come first. The daily tasks and pressures of raising a family can stress a relationship and start to take precedence over the couple's needs. Then, when one person or the other is too tired or unmotivated to have sex, it creates distance between even high-functioning partners. This is the beginning of a new normal that most couples want to avoid.

Still, 36% of the couples with kids manage to have sex three to four times a week, compared to 41% for those without kids. While

Frequency of Sex for Those with Kids Versus Those Without Kids

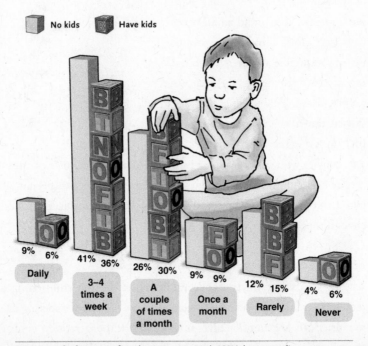

No kids   Have kids

	Daily	3–4 times a week	A couple of times a month	Once a month	Rarely	Never
No kids	9%	41%	26%	9%	12%	4%
Have kids	6%	36%	30%	9%	15%	6%

Percentages for frequency of sex do not sum to exactly 100% due to rounding.

both the frequency and perhaps the excitement of sexual passion slow down, the majority of parents continue to have active sex lives.

We know from other studies that sexual frequency does go down after the first child is born and may take a year or more to revive. And there is evidence that it never quite rises to the frequency that life together before children permitted. But if the sexless period post-childbirth goes on so long that the other partner is hurt or angry, it might be reasonable to see a counselor together to find out what is inhibiting the sexual connection.

Satisfaction with frequency of sex

Most men want more sex. In fact, twice as many men (60%) as women (30%) feel they're not getting enough. Moreover, 14% of women told us their partners want *too much* sex, while only 4% of men voiced that complaint. The rest—36% of men and 56% of women— said their frequency is just about right.

If we look at the international scene, some countries stand out in terms of more sexual activity than America, and their couples also have fewer complaints. Italy is one of the European sex stars, according to our study; significantly more Italians than Americans have sex three to four times a week.

How should we feel about relationships where there are lower rates of sexual interaction? Well, any rate of sexual interaction would be fine if everyone said they were happy with

> ## Who's Having the Most Sex
>
> *62% of couples in **Italy** have sex several times a week.*

it. But our findings indicate that only a third of all men think the amount of sex they get is just right and only slightly half of women are fully satisfied with the frequency of their sex lives. That leaves a lot of people with a normal they'd like to change. Committed couples need to be able to work out sexual compromises that please both partners.

Sexual obligation

Quantity and quality, of course, are two separate issues. When one or both partners have sex out of a sense of obligation rather than desire, they're not likely to rank that sex very high in quality. This is significantly more of a problem for women than for men. Thirty-one percent of women told us they often have sex out of obligation, compared to 16% of men. Moreover, this is no secret between partners. When we flipped the tables and asked people to describe their partners' motivation in having sex, 53% percent of men and 18% of women said their partners often had sex out of obligation.

Now, obligation isn't all bad if one partner is willingly trying to make the other happy. But if one partner is always or often going through the motions without getting much out of the experience, then sex becomes alienating instead of bonding. What's to be done? In some cases, the solution may be as simple as showing the passion and enthusiasm you truly feel. After all, more men *thought* their partners were having sex out of obligation than women admitted to. Or, if the desire for sex isn't there but the feelings of intense intimacy are, then both partners can still show that they love being close. However, if one partner honestly gets little or no satisfaction out of sex, then both partners need to establish a new normal.

Going to bed nude

We were surprised to find that only 34% of women and 38% of men said they sleep in the nude on a regular basis. As you'd expect, there seems to be some correlation between sleeping in the nude and sexual satisfaction. When your partner crawls into bed wearing flannel pajamas, the chances of being turned on and feeling intimate aren't as high as when he or she crawls into bed naked, especially if you are, too! And indeed, when we looked at the individuals who said they were *not* sexually satisfied, we found that 75% said they *never* sleep in the nude (though perhaps some people, not finding sex with their partners satisfying to begin with, don't want to encourage amorous thoughts).

Spontaneous kissing

Take note: *If you want to be more sexually satisfied, kiss more!* We know that kissing is an essential building block of sexual and emotional connection. And from what we've learned about women's need for intimacy and the need to have the right emotional context for lovemaking, a lot of kissing might be a good idea, assuming the kiss is a mutually affectionate experience. Yet only about 44% of women and 34% of men said they are often spontaneously kissed when not making love.

WANTED: MORE KISSES!

24% of men said their partners never *kiss them outside of actual lovemaking.*

Only 13% of men and women who are extremely sexually unsatisfied said they give spontaneous kisses! The absence of kissing as an affectionate rather than a sexual act could be a danger sign in a relationship.

Kissing lessons

We also asked men and women to rate their partners' kissing on a 1 to 10 scale. While the majority of respondents liked their partners' kisses, only 37% of women and 27% of men gave their partners a 9 or a 10 for their kissing score. The exceptions were Latin lovers, who received top scores from more than half of women we polled in Latin America!

Top Kisser

*52% of women and 46% of men in **Latin America** said their partners are a 9 or perfect 10!*

Alas, about one-fifth of all men and women rated their partners as a 5 or lower. Perhaps men want their norms raised to more passionate kissing, or perhaps women want more tenderness or passion in their kissing. We don't know from our data how individuals came up with their scores, but we suspect that just experimenting with different kinds of kisses—hard, soft, passionate, and tender—might cause ratings to soar.

"After a good movie, with a hot guy in it, I may for a moment fantasize about the hot guy while making love with my husband, but it's only for a couple seconds. . . . I'm sure I'm not the only one who does this." —female, 49, married 22 years, with kids

Sexual Fantasies

There has to have been a time, even if just for a millisecond, when you thought of someone other than your partner while making love. So, you might wonder, just how normal is it to have sexual fantasies? In our study, 53% of men said they sometimes think about someone else when making love. However, 38% of women also admitted to wandering thoughts!

The more important question is, if you occasionally imagine making love to someone else while with your partner, does this mean you're more likely to be *unsatisfied* with your real partner? No, there's zero correlation with satisfaction in the relationship or with sexual intimacy. It doesn't matter what age you are, either, or even how long you've been together. And it's also normal for happy couples to fantasize about sexual acts that their morals or ethics won't allow in real life. Our fantasies can break taboos that our actions never will.

What do we secretly want?

"I want to feel super-intimate. I want to have every part of my body touched and kissed. I want a lot of oral stimulation and sexual tension before getting into the act. I like having hard, rough sex, but I want passion and intimacy more so." —female, 23, committed relationship, no kids

Have you ever seen a movie with a sex scene so erotic that it makes you want to reenact the moves at home? Or do such movie scenes bring you down because you can't imagine you and your partner ever getting that steamy? How often do you share these reactions with your partner?

Movies and TV programs can set high expectations with their depictions of passionate sexuality, uninhibited coupling, being adored and desperately wanted, and pleasing and being pleased by a partner at the highest level of ecstasy. When people believe that their sexual or romantic relationship should play out the way relationships do in the media, there's a good chance they'll be severely disappointed. In fact, 43% of men told us they've watched sex scenes in movies or TV programs that make them feel bad about their own sex lives. More than a third of women (37%) have had the same experience. Most of these men and women know that the images they see are rare in long-term couples, but they want them anyhow.

The sad thing is that this disappointment is often needless. Men's and women's fantasies actually overlap quite a bit, and if they just shared them with their partners, they could improve their sex lives dramatically, to mutual benefit. But as long as people depend on their partners to *guess* what they want, few of these fantasies will ever get realized. Opening up a little can make all the difference.

My number-one sexual fantasy is . . .

When we asked, "What is your number-one sexual fantasy?" men normally included their wife or girlfriend. Most didn't appear to fantasize much about strangers or other women, except in a threesome. Interestingly, while men have a reputation for always dreaming about a threesome, that's also women's favorite fantasy—except that women want to have two *men* in bed with them. Women are loyal in their fashion, however: Many said the best threesome they could imagine would be with their husband and a clone of their husband. Actually, several men said the same about their wives. However, men were far more likely to incorporate kinky details into their fantasies than women.

Some particulars from both men and women:

"Giving my wife an orgasm while she talks dirty. She wants sex at least three times per week."—male, 50, married 21 years, with kids

"Mutual oral sex (69) to completion—wife then open-mouth kisses me. Or intercourse to completion and then wife pushes my head to perform oral sex on her."—male, 44, married 16 years, with kids

"Two men other than my husband pleasing me while my husband watches."—female, 25, married 5 years, with kids

"Me and two men, one taking me from behind, the other going down on me."—female, 34, married 12 years, no kids

"For my wife to dress very provocatively and we go out to dinner and drinks. Come home to an empty house, and she begins to make out with me and undress. Then she ties me up and teases me for a long time. She sits on my face and I lick her until she comes. She uses a strap-on on me, and then we make love."—male, 34, married 8 years, no kids

"Being passionately pushed up against a wall and ravished."—female, 40, married 15 years, with kids

"Red pumps, red lipstick, red bra and panties, eyeglasses, and an incredible blow job that ends in a beautiful facial."—male, 47, separated, seriously dating 6 months, with kids

"I want to watch my wife put on a masturbation show for me then we have additional foreplay, then finally intercourse." —male, 51, married 21 years, with kids

"I would be interested in dressing up as a 1940s Hollywood glamour girl and having sex with my partner in the shower." —female, 29, 3-year committed relationship, no kids

"To have my partner and me role-play, with him kidnapping me and me being his objectified sex slave." —female, 28, married 5 years, with kids

"Bondage sex with my wife." —male, 65, married 25 years, with kids

"Going to a topless bar with my boyfriend and wearing a long skirt/dress with no underwear on underneath. I eventually sit in his lap at our table. When I sit, I make sure to sit in his lap without the skirt or dress being between my private parts and his lap. Discreetly, we have sex in the bar, surrounded by other guests and entertainers." —female, 36, 6-month committed relationship, with kids

"Watching my wife get screwed by another man. When it's over, I tell her she's been a bad girl and I have passionate sex with her and feel like I've dominated her sexually." —male, 53, married 20 years, with kids

"My girlfriend and I are into S&M, but not as much as I would like. I'd like to get into latex and more severe restraints." —female, 25, 5-year relationship

"Hacer el amor perdidos en una casa de campo, rodeados de nieve, al calor de una chimenea, escuchando jazz. Tumbados en una alfombra frente a la chimenea. Probar cualquier postura sin censura amándonos toda la noche." (English translation: *"Making love, lost in a country house, surrounded by snow, enveloped in the warmth from the fireplace, listening to jazz. Lying on a carpet in front of the fireplace. Trying every position without censorship, loving all night."*)—male from Spain, 41, married 13 years

Fantasy role-playing

Unless it's Halloween, most couples find it awkward to dress up and engage in sexual role-playing. Only 16% of our respondents overall said they do it, find it satisfying, and feel it helps their relationships. However, when we narrowed our focus to just the couples who are most satisfied sexually, we found that nearly *one-fourth* of these extremely satisfied couples incorporate role-playing into their sex lives. As one man said, *"When we go into our roles (I am the cowboy and she is the daughter of the ranch owner), it always ends up hotter than when we have regular sex."*

Are all those other couples missing a bet? Maybe, but it doesn't seem likely that role-playing will become much more popular for the majority. Easy availability of erotic costumes notwithstanding, it's difficult for most people to take on the persona of sexy teacher, naughty nurse, or macho cowboy and sustain the pretense without feeling ridiculous or

ACTING ON FANTASY

24% of couples who are extremely satisfied sexually incorporate role-playing into their sex lives.

giggling. Role-playing requires quite a bit of confidence and comfort with the fantasy element of sexuality.

This comfort level seems to be slightly higher in the gay community, where 30% of men who are very satisfied sexually also participate in role-playing. Perhaps it's true that when one norm is challenged others can also be questioned and modified. Quite a few years ago there was a group called the Village People who had a hit song, "Y.M.C.A." When they sang it, they were dressed as a police officer, a construction worker, an Indian, a GI, a cowboy, and a biker. The point of the costumes was that you could be anything you wanted to be erotically, and why not? In fact, the group's performance made another deeper suggestion: that erotic feelings are very individualized, sometimes unique, and that we might even think of sexual diversity as normal. Any sexual fantasy or act that's appealing to one person may turn off another, but those differences are differences in taste, not differences in mental health. Role-playing may not be common, but it is normal as long as the fantasies involved aren't preludes to acts that threaten any children or unconsenting adults.

Better Lover

"I'm a better lover due to my maturity . . . As a young lover, the focus tended to be more on my own satisfaction or orgasm. Now my focus is on my partner and making certain he loves every minute with me . . . it's such a turn-on to see the excitement in him because I care so much about pleasing him to the max. It not only makes it better for him, but for myself as well. I also know exactly how to move and position myself to achieve deep, sensual penetration, no

"... and this is my bedroom."

matter what position we are in. I'm also more open about touching and using my mouth and trusting my husband enough to do whatever he wishes."—female, 59, married with adult children

It's not easy for most people to talk to their partners about their sexual needs and preferences. Even when there are significant problems, such as ineffective foreplay, premature ejaculation, or phobic reactions against sex in general or one act in particular, men and women are often afraid to broach the subject, afraid that they'll seem to be accusing the other person of inadequacy. If the desire is to exchange or enact certain fantasies, even a long-married partner might be afraid of being received with disgust, boredom, or criticism.

There are good reasons for this timidity. If the partner reacts with anger or embarrassment, it can create or worsen problems. Not wanting to risk the tension or rejection, many people keep their desires and frustrations to themselves. Still, if the fantasy is something they used to enjoy in another relationship, or the way things are playing out now isn't satisfying, the hidden feelings can fester into a sense of deprivation or resentment.

It's worth considering that a very large number of men who visit prostitutes are married and, while they go for all kinds of reasons, many are driven by the desire for some specific sexual act (like giving or receiving oral sex) that isn't available at home. To bring more awareness to these unmet needs, we gave men and women a long list of choices and asked them to pick the top two things they feel are missing from their sexual relationship. We listed everything from "wishing my partner had better hands" to "wishing my partner had better body odor." Here's what they told us. . . .

Men speak out: My partner could be a better lover if . . .

The Normal Bar showed that almost a third of men (30%) want their partners to do different sexual acts. Men complain that sex with their partners is always predictable. Even if they are part of the problem, predictable sex isn't what a substantial number of them really want. It's not that these men are necessarily unhappy, they just want to mix things up a bit, perhaps with additional positions, new kinds of foreplay, or the other partner initiating sex more often.

The second most common wish among men (22%) was for their partners to be less passive—and more passionate. These men want their sex lives to go outside the bounds of usual excitement. Of course, the men who checked wanting less predictability and more variety also, indirectly, are asking for more passion.

The third item on men's most-wanted list is more sexual feedback from their partners. Sixteen percent said they would like to hear more sexual noises from their partners, sounds to let them know that their partners are enjoying the experience. In other words, positive reinforcement and encouragement.

Our findings square with other studies about sexuality in couples. The sexual beginning of most lasting relationships is intense and passionate. Women are responsive, focused, and excited. Men feel sexually strong and effective, and are thrilled to drive their partners "wild." As time goes by and couples get used to each other, however, the sexual temperature may go from hot to warm (and in troubled couples, to cold). In a good relationship that's not all there is, but men still say they miss it, especially when the media remind them what those most passionate periods are like. They want their partners to go wild again and surprise them. They want to feel like the best lovers their partners have ever had or could have. It's a lot to expect after twenty years together, but a substantial number of men would love it.

WHAT MEN WANT FROM THEIR PARTNERS

#1: Sexual Diversity
(new sexual acts)
#2: Less Passivity
(more passion)
#3: Sexual Noises
(more feedback)

WHAT WOMEN WANT FROM THEIR PARTNERS

#1: Foreplay
(more touching)
#2: Romance
(more loving passion)
#3: Less Predictability
(more spontaneous and fun)

Women speak out: My partner could be a better lover if . . .

A long time ago a psychologist named Terry Tafoya used to joke, "The reason that some women fake orgasm is that some men fake foreplay." Well, it's no joke that women's top desire in our study was for more foreplay. One-quarter of our women said they don't get enough of it. They want to be touched more.

The second item on women's wish list is sexual romance and passion. Twenty percent of women want more passion; but, of course, if they were more aroused in the early stages of lovemaking, that wish might become moot.

Number three for 19% of women mirrored men's wish for less predictability and more diversity. It appears that men and women both want more novelty, but no one's taking the initiative. The Normal Bar data say, go for it!

New Normal Advice

After dating for five years, Letty and Paul were on the road to marriage, but they'd never told each other their sexual fantasies until we told them about the Normal Bar data. Both in their early thirties, they were a little uncertain about this exercise, but once they spoke up they were relieved to find that their number-one and number-two sexual fantasies involved each other! Letty told Paul that, as silly as it might sound, she thought it would be very sexy for him to hold her up with her legs wrapped around his waist and her back against the wall while they kissed and made love. She'd seen that in a movie once and thought about it from time to time. Paul confided that he often thought about doing the 69 position (which they'd rarely tried) and playing with sex toys. They had fun talking about their fantasies and opening up with each other and left it at that.

Then, on Letty's birthday, Paul took her to Las Vegas for the weekend. They enjoyed a special dinner and a show. That night, back in the hotel room, Paul made Letty's number-one fantasy come true. It was just the way she imagined it, and she felt incredibly loved and connected to Paul because he'd remembered her desire for this particular sex act. He'd actually planned it as part of her birthday treat! Letty was more than willing to bring Paul's fantasy to life too.

Letting go of inhibitions and losing control with one another is scary for many of us. It is amazing how constrained sexual intimacy can be, even when we have the security of a truly loving relationship. What can help us get past our fear? The first part of the answer always involves communication. Most desire is unspoken. Even long-term couples may be embarrassed to ask for and explain what they want and why. But talk is a vital form of foreplay.

The second part of the answer involves detaching from inhibition. Many of us have been taught that experiencing wild abandon, including rougher sex or exotic acts, is shameful or somehow wrong. It might seem offensive even to suggest trying them, but unless we do we may be shortchanging our erotic potential: Squeamishness and prudishness make chilling bedfellows.

The first step is to ask for what you want: Tell your partner what you're thinking. Research indicates that gay men are rather expert at this, compared to everyone else. Perhaps this is because men better understand each other's needs. Or perhaps it's because sex isn't as taboo a topic among gay men, and this helps couples to be direct, share fantasies, and create a mutual sexual itinerary. This does not mean that all gay couples agree on what they want, but it does make for fewer inhibitions about discussing and trying new possibilities. If you keep your intimate sexual thoughts a secret, your sexual relationship has no chance to improve.

Tool 40 ▶ Learn Your Partner's Favorite Fantasy and Consider It!

This tool could be as simple as asking your partner what his or her most erotic fantasy is. Just sharing that information would be new to most couples, and could be fun. If you have good communication and trust in your relationship, it could add a lot more to your sex life.

Even if the fantasy is too extreme to actually try, you could playact it in your bedroom. For example, if he fantasizes about a three-way, and neither of you would feel comfortable actually doing that, you could pretend there was a third person present, use a mirror, or watch a video of a three-way and use that as an arousal device.

Tool 41 ▶ The Great Sex Weekend

Not sure what new adventures would suit your comfort zone? Start with a book such as Anne Hooper's gorgeously explicit volumes, like *The Ultimate Sex Guide*, which show sexual positions and possibilities. Or check out *The Great Sex Weekend*, which suggests ways to put romance and eroticism together on a getaway weekend. Read it with your partner, and each of you can highlight suggestions that interest you. Then discuss what you've marked, and try some of the ideas you both find interesting. Who knows? You might feel differently about the things that didn't appeal to you after a few new experiences.

TOOL 42 ▶ Kissing All Over—Literally

Kiss all over. Start from the top and kiss every bit of real estate. Take turns, front and back. . . . Tell your partner which kisses are the most thrilling ("Do that again!").

TOOL 43 ▶ Dim the Lights

Put dimmers on your bedroom lights. If you already have them, change the color of the bulbs. Or do both! Then turn the lights down, turn on the music, and chill the champagne as a surprise announcement of your intentions for the evening.

TOOL 44 ▶ Surprise Night

Set a night once a month to try something in bed that you've never done or haven't done in a long time. It could be as simple as making love on the floor instead of the bed, putting perfume on in unusual places, wearing something you would not generally wear, or wearing nothing at all.

Chapter 12

Secrets and Lies

"Hey, isn't that your wife?"
"Yes, just ignore her . . . we have a bit of a trust issue."

Trust matters. Among extremely happy couples, only 7% of men and women harbor doubts about their partner's honesty and fidelity. But when trust fails, paranoia can ruin even otherwise perfect relationships.

Accusers typically feel righteous, as well as hurt, when they suspect a deception. However, people often misdirect their accusations and fears. If you've been cheated on in a previous relationship, you may bring that mistrust to your current one even if your present mate is devoted, honest, and true. It's understandable; yet, unwarranted suspicion can infect and damage the relationship.

When honor and integrity are questioned, especially if the suspicions are unfounded, the person accused of misdeeds is generally furious. Even if the suspicions are completely warranted, the accused may be furious that his or her defense hasn't worked! In fact, the need to be trusted is so basic that even repeat liars will become indignant when accused. Even when caught in the act, the cheater may protest, "How dare you not trust me!"

The answer is: easily. The Normal Bar data show us that *even in good relationships*, trust is shaky. Having complete and total confidence in a partner seems to be a struggle for most of us.

Perhaps some of this caution comes from self-knowledge. If we doubt our own trustworthiness or feel guilty about our own indiscretions, we're more likely to project that doubt onto our partner. Everyone has insecurities, but if they get out of hand and turn into paranoia, they can have a terrible effect on a relationship.

Do you trust your partner?

Only 39% of women in this study completely trust their partners, compared to 53% of men. What's wrong with this picture? Why the gender difference, and why the low levels of trust in general? It may be that a lot of couples intuitively know or have learned by experience that their spouse or live-in partner has the potential to rove.

Women in heterosexual relationships know the same thing that many studies have shown: that men are more interested in and titillated about sex outside the relationship, and that may account for a higher percentage of women who doubt their partner's honesty and fidelity. On the other hand, nearly half of men suspect their partners, too. Both men and women believe that their partners

> **COUPLES BEWARE**
>
> *Only 53% of men and 39% of women completely trust their partners.*

Doesn't Trust Partner

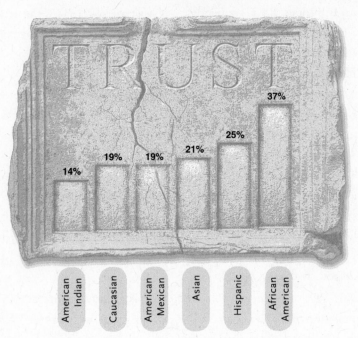

will hide unpleasant truths, and that they may have to dig to find out what is really going on.

When we look at trust and compare how it functions among different ethnic groups, we do find some variation. African Americans are less likely to fully trust their partners than are members of other ethnicities we surveyed.

Do you have feelings of jealousy?

Feelings of jealousy can be a measure of relationship insecurity. Our data show that women (40%) feel more jealous than men (23%). Perhaps this is because both genders believe that men are more likely to stray than women. It could also reflect the statistical reality that, should the relationship break up, the man is more likely to find another partner. This is particularly true in some African American communities, where the ratio of available women to men skews dramatically in favor of men. In all cultures, however, women are more vulnerable if they have children and if they have low or no independent income. These comparative vulnerabilities help us understand the gender differential in jealousy.

It is interesting, however, to note that the Normal Bar shows more than twice as much jealousy among 18-to-24-year-olds (55%) than among people in their fifties (24%). That is likely because relationships are in a lot more jeopardy when people are young and often still restless, unmarried, and childless. Individuals in their late teens and early twenties tend to have shorter investments in each other, and lots more contact with enticing and eligible alternative partners. In these younger age groups, jealousy is often justified.

The level of jealousy in most relationships, however, is harmless and does not affect mutual happiness or sexual satisfaction. While continuing distrust and overactive suspicions can undermine feelings of unity and respect over time, becoming toxic and even dangerous, a little jealousy every now and then can be flattering. Everything in moderation!

What Causes Partners to Lie?

People lie in relationships because they're afraid of the reaction they'd get if they told the truth. They weigh the pros and cons, and if lying will save them some grief, they often take the low road. However, few men and women feel good about lying, especially when they get caught!

What exactly constitutes a lie? Deception can be as black-and-white as telling your partner you've been at the store when actually you've been having coffee with a former lover. Other lies are "gray," meant to spare hurt feelings or sidestep unnecessary discussions. Common gray lies, for example, downplay or withhold information about past lovers that the current partner doesn't need—or really want—to know.

Other lies exaggerate or put a spin on true stories. Some people habitually invent or enlarge reality—either consciously or unconsciously. Over time, their partners learn to discount what they hear. Their emotional reaction then depends on the subject matter. "I'll be home in five minutes" is irritating when it turns out to be a lie, but it is not a conflagration if someone becomes aware over time that their

"You look nice. Is that a new dress?"
"Oh no, I've had this old thing forever."

partner is usually an hour late. On the other hand, when a partner says, "I only had one glass of wine," the stakes change if the amount was actually a whole bottle of wine. That lie has serious consequences and discovery is likely to cause a much more intense reaction.

Have you ever lied to your partner?

Nearly three-quarters of our respondents (75% of men and 71% of women) said they lie to their partners to one degree or another. Only 27% of our respondents said they never ever lie. Does lying negatively affect the quality of your relationship? Probably not. Even among extremely happy couples, 69% of men and women said they've lied at some point to their partners.

But the fact that very happy partners lie demands some further scrutiny. For most couples, some lying is necessary to keep the peace, to protect each other's feelings, and to preserve a sense of safety in the relationship. The 27% who never lie may be righteous, but they can also be cruelly frank. Men and women who shade the truth may be more loving and protective. Even well-intentioned lies, however, can hurt the relationship if the truth that's withheld is something the partner has every right and need to know. Knowing when a lie is reasonable and when it is reprehensible isn't always an easy call.

INTERNATIONAL CHECKPOINT

In which country do people lie to their partners the *least* compared to people in other countries?

Only half the men and women in **Hungary** said they lie to their partners.

Have you ever lied about prices on clothes or other products?

More than a third (36%) of women and 19% of men told us they've lied about the cost of a product. Lying about the cost of something doesn't appear to have any direct negative effects on the relationship, but lying about even as small a thing as the cost of a dress is definitely not a habit you want to get into. It's not worth losing the trust of your partner over an article of clothing that you say cost $50 when he or she can easily learn that the true price was $250.

Have you ever lied about how your partner looks?

Lying about how your partner looks is definitely a white lie, and a common one among men. Forty percent of men and 24% of women lie to their partners about appearance. The gender disparity is probably due to the fact that women more frequently *ask* how they look and are more likely to want reassurance that they look great. Men correctly gauge that very few women want to be criticized about their looks, and so they give the kind answer, if not necessarily the truthful one.

Have you ever lied about how much money you have?

People are often more secretive about money than anything else. One-fourth of all women and men lie to their partners about money. Even spouses will exaggerate how much or how little cash they have. You might think that lying about your net worth or how much you have in the bank would cause big problems, but surprisingly, for the majority of couples in our study, it does not. And, curiously, of our various religious categories, religious Christians, including Catholics and mainline as well as evangelical Protestants, lead non-believers and Jewish partners in this form of economic deception!

Do you lie about your feelings?

Relationships are *supposed to be* open, sharing, and honest. But 59% of men and 56% of women lie about their feelings. Half of all partners not only stifle their emotions but also give misleading feedback about what's going on in their head and heart. As you might guess, people who are less happy lie the most. In fact, 72% of unhappy partners

Have Lied to Their Partners about How Much Money They Have

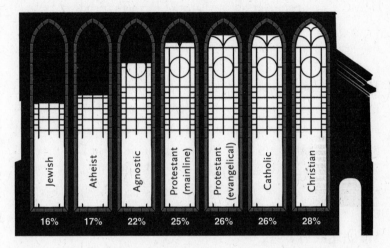

Jewish	Atheist	Agnostic	Protestant (mainline)	Protestant (evangelical)	Catholic	Christian
16%	17%	22%	25%	26%	26%	28%

choose not to share their true feelings with their partners. Whether this emotional deception is a cause or an effect of the overall unhappiness, it makes it very difficult to fix the relationship. The surprising finding, however, is that 48% of extremely happy partners also lie about their feelings.

Do you lie about what your friends and family really say and think?

Nearly a third (31%) of all women and 28% of men lie about what their friends and family really think. Age and duration of the relationship make no difference here. We think many people are protecting their partners from criticism, which is a reasonable thing to do; but of course it doesn't let their partners know who is really a supporter or who is undermining the relationship with critical comments about them. However, it may be the only way to keep peace in the valley or preserve relationships with friends and family that would be discouraged or forbidden if a partner really knew what was being said about him or her. Of course, now that you know this statistic, you might be a bit paranoid about what your partner's friends and family really think of you—but remember, the majority of partners do not lie—or do not need to lie.

Do you lie about your partner's sexual performance?

Just as men are more likely to tell white lies about their partner's appearance, women are more likely to flatter their partner's sexual performance. We found that 43% of women lie about how they feel about their partner's sexual performance, compared to just 28% of men. That's probably not because women are better lovers but, rather, because they feel a greater need to protect their partner's feelings. When a man feels insecure, he may have difficulty getting an erection, so it's in his partner's—as well as his—interest to boost his sexual self-esteem. The bad news here is that some honest communication has to take place; otherwise, nothing is likely to improve.

WANT BETTER SEX?

You and your partner will both enjoy sex more if you talk more openly about what you aren't *getting and what you really* need.

Who lies the *most* about sexual performance? At first glance it looks like the longer couples are together, the more likely they are to lie. In the first year, only 24% of men and women say they lie to their partners about their sexual performance. By six to nine years, that number has risen to 46%. Over time, however, many couples realize they need more honest communication between the sheets. After twenty years together, the percentage of sexual fibbers drops to 39%. This is a smaller but not inconsequential number of men and women who mislead their lovers.

As you might imagine, sexually dissatisfied men and women lie almost twice as much (50%) as sexually satisfied partners (27%). If you talk openly and honestly with your partner about what isn't working, you're much more likely to achieve sexual satisfaction than if you salve your partner's sexual feelings at the expense of your own pleasure. Lying may cause fewer storms, but also fewer orgasms!

Here are a few typical lies about sexual performance:

"That he's big and made me orgasm." —female, 30, married, no kids

"In the days when we did have sex, I told her she was great." —male, 60, married, no kids

"He asked me (in the middle of sex) if he was 'the best.' Of course I said yes. He's not, but the one who was better was also an arrogant rat-bastard." —female, 44, married, no kids

"I lied when I said I enjoyed sex, but I really didn't. All she cares about is how she can get done with me; but I do whatever is necessary to make sure she is pleased." —male, 62, married, no kids

"Sometimes when I am really tired and I just want him to finish, I pretend to climax." —female, 50, divorced, no kids

"I tell her the blow job was great when it really sucked." —male, 60, married, no kids

"Giving me orgasms through intercourse—it's very difficult for me and I didn't want to make him feel bad." —female, 23, never married, in a 5-year relationship, no kids

"I suggested I was more turned on than I was."—male, 45, married, with kids

"Circumference <u>does</u> matter. He isn't wide or long. But I tell him it is perfect."—female, 54, in a relationship, no kids

Do you lie about your past sexual experiences?

Most couples tell each other the truth about their past sexual liaisons. However, 28% of women and 31% of men lie about them. Some of these lies may be intended to spare their partner's feelings. Others may be told to make the liar seem more promiscuous or experienced than he or she really is. The risk is always that the lie will be exposed, leaving the misled partner doubly aggrieved—by both the misinformation and the breach of trust. On the other hand, it appears that a lot of these prevarications never get exposed, because the Normal Bar shows that lying about past sexual experience has no effect on relationship happiness or sexual satisfaction.

Have you ever lied about where you've been?

A full half of all men and 36% of women said they sometimes lie about where they've been and what they've been doing. One of these respondents explained, "I have to admit, I lie by omission a lot of the time. For example, I don't tell Henry when I see my ex. He really doesn't like him and I think he thinks I've still got a thing for him. I don't, but I do want to keep a friendship going. So I either don't tell Henry or I tell him I am with my girlfriends when I am really meeting my ex for dinner."

Here's another example: "I tell her I work late but I really only work late some of the time. My coworkers and I go out for a few beers now and then. I don't tell her where I am. She would be on me for that and I'd just as soon avoid having to handle her reaction. So I just tell her I'm working and I don't have a big argument."

While most people might give a functional rationale like the two above, the fact is, more unhappy than happy people lie about where they've been. More than half (51%) of people who are extremely unhappy lie about their whereabouts, compared to 33% of those who are extremely happy. It may also be the case that some of those lies have to do with sex, since 56% of those who are sexually dissatisfied lie about where they've been compared to only 28% of those who are sexually satisfied.

Have you read your partner's e-mail?

Privacy seems to be in jeopardy. More than half (54%) of women and 49% of men read their partner's e-mail! It doesn't matter if they're happy or unhappy with their relationships, either. Anyone, it seems, can be tempted to sneak a peek at private messages.

It may be that a lot of couples keep their computers open and their e-mail accessible. However, that doesn't constitute an open invitation. One man said, "I caught my girlfriend going through my e-mail and I went wild. How dare she do that! It just eroded any trust I had in her. We broke up over it. When I started dating Georgia [his wife] I told her about that incident because I wanted to make sure she knew how strongly I felt about my privacy."

PRIVATE SPIES

Anywhere from 40% to 60% of people around the globe said they've read through some of their partner's e-mails.

New Normal Advice

Judith had been in a relationship with a partner she was sure was cheating on her, and it made her crazy. This turbulent history and the constant betrayals not only caused the end of that relationship but also infected her subsequent relationship with Billy. Her jealousy and lack of trust made Billy crazy too. He caught her going through his pockets, his desk, and his phone. He eventually broke up with her because of it, and she never did find out if her suspicions were correct.

Years later she fell in love with Stuart. She told him about the earlier turmoil and her tendency to be paranoid with men she cared about. It turned out that her hypersensitivity stemmed not only from her boyfriends' behavior but also from her father's infidelity to her mother. Stuart asked what it would take for her to trust him. She thought about it and she said, "No secrets." To her, this meant an open computer with no secret passwords, never being anyplace she couldn't contact him on a land phone, and no repeating lunches, dinners, or business trips with attractive women.

Stuart was willing to meet all those conditions and then some. Not only did Judith stop being suspicious and jealous, but she ultimately relaxed some of her conditions. They eventually married and, according to Stuart, her jealousy has never been an issue again.

Deception and dishonesty often reflect insecurity, but they also represent a breach of trust. While lies can seem like an easy way out, they probably trap more liars than they help, and most take their toll on a relationship. Once you start lying you have to keep the façade up, and it's not easy to remember all the details of a story that never happened! Furthermore, you're bound to wonder what your partner will think of you if and when the truth comes out.

Lying erodes intimacy. Even if your partner believes the deception, you know who you really are and what you're doing, so the lie inevitably becomes a wedge between you. It stops you from facing issues and having the hard conversations that every couple needs to have in order to grow and change for the better.

Tool 45 ▶ Trigger Points

We all have trigger points to one degree or another. Maybe your jealousy flares up when your partner dresses a certain way or talks to the opposite sex too long in a social setting. Many of us, like Judith, need to recognize these triggers before we can get past them, and sometimes it's best to spell them out to yourself and to your partner.

Have a conversation with your partner about each of your respective "trust buttons." Tell each other why you think you have certain exposed nerves. Was it a past relationship? Family history? Knowing and understanding each other's most sensitive vulnerabilities can elevate intimacy, enabling you to protect your partner's weak spots. Working hard not to push the buttons that create anger and fear can change undesirable emotions and reactivity so much that those issues cease to be a problem, and a new normal emerges.

Tool 46 ▶ Agree to Not Tell Everything

You may feel compelled to lie if your partner wants to know details that would hurt, such as how many sexual partners you've actually had. Talk about why it's not productive to go over the sexual past and agree not to ask these kinds of questions yourself. Figure out that there is no upside to that kind of information.

**TOOL 47 ▶ Turn to Counseling If You're Insecure,
Not to Your Partner's E-mail**

If you're searching your partner's e-mail for clues about what
he or she is thinking or saying when you're apart, you have a
problem that you need to address. You obviously don't feel
secure about your partner's affections or loyalty, and finding
hurtful information will only deepen that insecurity. A better
idea is to strengthen the relationship so that you feel confident your partner would not betray you or want to say intimate things to someone else.

     This is easy to say, but sometimes very hard to do. If
you're reduced to going through your partner's pockets and
e-mail to find out if he or she still loves you or is loyal to you,
it's probably time to see a therapist or counselor. With professional help you can find out if your paranoia has some basis
to it, or if your insecurity has other causes. A good therapist
will be able to figure out whether it is a couples issue or a
personal one.

TOOL 48 ▶ The Direct Approach to Sexual Truth

Instead of lying to pump up your partner's libido, suggest
some new approaches that will give you a neutral starting
point. For example, "Why don't we try a gentle stroking
when we first start making love? I think I'm getting into tender touches. What would you like?" Then show honest enthusiasm when your partner does what you like, and either
don't respond or suggest an adjustment when it's not working for you. Try to cultivate accurate as well as encouraging
feedback.

CHAPTER 13

Unfaithful

Temptations

"I have a huge crush on a friend of mine, and it's mutual. It enhances my life enormously, and although I feel I have every right to enjoy it, I feel no impetus to share it with my spouse." —female, 33, married 10 years

According to the Normal Bar data, total fidelity of mind as well as body is the rare exception. It's not abnormal to be tempted to stray. However, for many people this temptation poses a moral dilemma. In Western society men and women prize the freedom to mingle freely, yet this easy access to members of the opposite sex can raise anxiety in our partners and in ourselves. No one is policing our every movement, so we have to be responsible for our own reactions when our hormones start percolating. For some, this responsibility is a real burden.

Why are fantasies about sex outside one's primary relationship so common? In part because lust is the key to our species' survival, as it is for most animals. Geese are the only species we know of that pair only once during a lifetime; if one mate dies, the bereft partner stays unmatched until death. This is not a great model for repopulating the species, so humans have developed a strong sex drive that isn't limited to one partner. Being able to imagine sex with alternative partners prepares us to start over in the event of death or divorce. In a sense, then, we need those fantasies of infidelity. On the other hand, because we've promised to be faithful, and because we know the likely and unpleasant consequences if we break that promise, most of us constrain ourselves to looking without touching.

Sexually fantasizing about other people

Just meeting another person can arouse physical or emotional attraction. This response does not turn off just because you're in a committed relationship. The Normal Bar shows that 61% of women and 90% of men fantasize sexually about people they meet. There's no stopping imagination!

IMAGINARY LOVERS

61% of women and 90% of men fantasize sexually about people they meet.

Supporting the premise that this is an instinctive response—rather than a reflection on the primary relationship—we found no correlation between the duration of a relationship and the amount of lusting that goes on outside it. After your first year as a couple, you may or may not "lust in your heart" for others, but there's no reason to fear that your partner is daydreaming about others just because you've been together so long.

More surprisingly, the Normal Bar data also show virtually no connection between fantasies of infidelity and happiness in the core relationship. Temptation happens; it doesn't matter if you are unhappy or happy with your main squeeze.

Fantasizing about porn

When the topic of pornography comes up, a majority of women normally have a quick and negative reaction. While some women may enjoy erotic pictures and movies, they worry about their children seeing sleazy, dehumanizing photos of women or pictures of acts that are bizarre, illegal, or both. Still, pornography is titillating to both sexes, and sex sells.

SECRET VOYEURS

6% of women in the United States said, "Yes, I have watched porn alone."

A gigantic majority of 89% of our male respondents told us they enjoy porn. More than a quarter (28%) use it often; 17% from time to time; and 44% said they use some kind of pornographic material occasionally. So if you think your boyfriend or husband is kinky because he uses porn occasionally, think again. He shares a taste for erotic material with most other men.

While porn is mainly used by men, it isn't only used by men. However, while the majority of women (59%) who use pornography use it with their partners, the majority of men enjoy porn alone. And not always with their partners' knowledge. About 42% of women (as opposed to 15% of men) said they discovered their partners were secretly using porn.

Sex with anybody you wanted for one night

Still in the realm of fantasy, we wondered what some of the secret yearnings of men and women would be if there were no negative consequences for their sexual trespasses. So we asked, "If you had the opportunity to have sex with anybody you wanted outside your current relationship and it would have zero effect on your current relationship or family, as if it never happened, would you do it?" Men went for this fantasy by a ratio of three to two over women! Two-thirds of men (65%) and just under half of women (43%) found this a compelling proposition.

This suggests that many of us harbor a secret longing for sexual adventure and romance, even if we never act on it. We don't want these attractions to undermine our relationship or our moral commitments, but still . . . we can't help thinking about that attractive new colleague at the company picnic.

Given the normalcy of these fantasies, we also wondered if our respondents thought their partners would have sex with somebody else if given the same free pass. The responses were remarkably accurate. Men were spot-on, with 43% of men predicting their partners would go for it; and 58% of women thought their mates would seize the opportunity.

It's one thing to be offered a "freebie," however, and another to actually plan, invite, or agree to sex outside the relationship. Some couples joke that each has given the other permission have sex with some cherished movie star (think: Sting, Katy Perry, George Clooney, Angelina Jolie, Brad Pitt, Charlize Theron, Taylor Lautner), but would that really happen if the unlikely encounter occurred? And what about going beyond fantasy with that new colleague at the picnic *in spite of* the repercussions? This is where extreme sexual dissatisfaction can make a difference in the response. Among our dissatisfied couples, 79% of men and 65% of women said they'd jump at the chance to have sex with somebody new for one night. People who are starving are more tempted to eat, even if it's "forbidden fruit." But having a very good sex life isn't a total safeguard; 53% of men and 28% of women who are fully satisfied with sex at home are still interested in the seductive stranger or Hollywood icon.

Would you consider sex outside your relationship with somebody who propositioned you?

We are now leaving the world of fantasy and looking at real reactions to actual opportunities. Not all temptation is in the eye of the beholder. Sometimes it takes the form of an overt proposition from the one beheld. And what happens then? Nearly half (48%) of women and two-thirds (69%) of men told us that if they were actually propositioned by someone they were attracted to outside their relationships they'd be tempted to act on it. It's a good thing people aren't more sexually forward, or we might have a lot more infidelity!

The Normal Bar does show that people who are more sexually satisfied are less likely to be tempted to have sex outside the relationship, but our overall finding here is that more overt invitations would equal more cheating. The best way to stay monogamous may be to keep your partner close when entrancing alternatives are near.

WHEN TEMPTATION STRIKES

48% of women and 69% of men said if they were propositioned to have sex by somebody they were attracted to outside their relationships, they would be tempted to act on it!

Do you think there is somebody better out there for you?

Why do so many people fantasize about alternative bedmates? Do they think there might be someone better out there than their current partner? Or are they actively looking for escape from bad sex at home? When we asked people who are either married or in a serious committed relationship if they thought there might be someone better for them than their current partner, 75% of those who didn't like their sex lives said yes, absolutely. That's a lot of people tempted to leave.

When we looked at those who are extremely satisfied with their sex lives, however, only 25% of them said they thought there was somebody out there who'd be even better for them than their current partner.

Duration of the relationship, curiously, has little or no connection to these results. It's not years together, or what sociologists call a "habituation effect," that determines how men and women view their sexual alternatives. Instead, the deciding factor seems to be sexual dissatisfaction, which corresponds to a number of undesirable relationship outcomes. A good sex life is critical, at least for the majority of couples, if the partners want to stay true to each other in their minds as well as their bodies.

Causes for Sexual Temptation

"Being married isn't what I expected. Our sex life is quite boring and I find myself longing for another relationship—more like how I imagined it."—female, 27, married 6 years, no kids

For some couples, diminishing communication, affection, and attraction can all contribute to the desire to stray. The Normal Bar shows that loss of sexual pleasure or frequency can make even

otherwise happy couples vulnerable. But where and how specifically are these temptations most likely to occur?

Close friends getting closer . . .

Are your friends your competition? Are you attracted to your partner's friends? An overwhelming 86% of men and 85% of women said they don't think they have any friends who tempt their partners. However, it appears that they are very much mistaken because, when we reversed the question, we found that nearly half (45%) of men and more than one-fourth (26%) of women in fact *are* attracted to friends of their partners and are tempted to act on it. This poses an uncomfortable dilemma, since most of us would like our partners to be friends with our friends—but not *intimate* friends.

The best defense is a good sexual offense. People who are extremely satisfied sexually are a lot less tempted to act on an outside

Too Close for Comfort?

45% of men and 26% of women said they are attracted to one of their partner's friends and are tempted to act on it!

attraction. While 52% of people who are unsatisfied with their sex lives responded that they would be tempted to act on an attraction outside of the relationship, only 17% of the people who are sexually satisfied said they'd be tempted.

Away on a business trip

Going away on a business trip might sound like fun if you don't travel much, but people who travel a great deal don't necessarily enjoy all the stress and lonely nights. After too many dinners alone or with nasty, tedious, or difficult clients, it can be a welcome counterpoint to meet someone attractive on the plane, at the airport, or at the hotel bar. Away from the watchful eyes of family, friends, and spouse, such meetings can also be seductive.

When we looked more closely at the group that cheated, we found that business trips were the most common settings for temptations that led to infidelity. More than one-third (36%) of men and 13% of women told us that they gave in to temptation on a business trip. The Normal Bar shows that, when broken out by years in a relationship, vulnerability to temptation during business trips increases greatly at six to nine years. This also happens to be the period when relationships are most fragile and need the most attention, so this isn't very surprising.

What is surprising is that it doesn't matter how happy these men and women were in their relationships or even how satisfied they were sexually at home. Some men and women just can't or don't want to resist a sexual opportunity that they're likely to get away with. It's

Gave into Sexual Temptation While Traveling

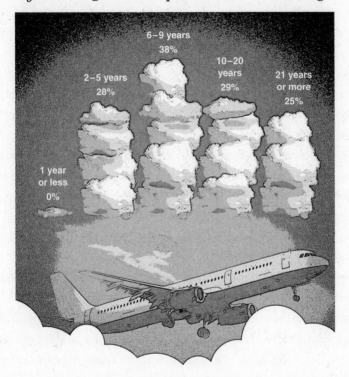

often easier to enhance the adventure of life, or one's ego, by a sexual liaison than to resist temptation, go back home, and figure out ways to make that life as thrilling as the opportunity.

Fell in love with someone else

There is a huge difference, of course, between one-night stands and full-blown love affairs. The latter normally happen to people who are already unhappy in their relationships. Nearly half (48%) of people who gave in to temptation while unhappy in their primary relationships said they'd fallen in love with the other person.

Only 20% of people who fell in love with somebody else had been in extremely happy relationships. But this minority raises an important question: How can someone who isn't just happy but *extremely* happy with his or her partner fall in love with someone else? Some people may be capable of loving, or wanting, more than one person at a time; some may unexpectedly meet another soul mate; and some have what they think will be a "harmless" sexual adventure that turns into something else. The sad truth is that these affairs often produce the most pain and turmoil because the partner at home, knowing and valuing the happiness and trust within the relationship, cannot imagine or comprehend the infidelity. When the truth comes out, devastation will follow.

Ran across an old flame

Here's a warning to men: When an old flame approaches your lady, watch out. Nearly one-third (32%) of women who admitted to acting on sexual temptation said it was with an old boyfriend or crush, compared to 21% of men. And the danger zone for this occurring is two to five years into a relationship, when the rate of old-flame affairs among the unfaithful jumps to 42%!

The Normal Bar reveals an additional alarm in that old flames are just as appealing to those who are in sexually satisfying and extremely happy relationships. So if you value your relationship and your partner's ex comes around, stay close and watchful. For quite a few people, old embers never totally die out.

Sexually bored

A mundane sex life may encourage your partner to have a fling that doesn't include you! Boredom was the reason 71% of unfaithful men and 49% of the women gave for acting on sexual temptation. Think

that your relationship is so good that
sexual boredom is no big deal? You
could be wrong. Even people who
are very happy in their relationships
admitted to curing their sexual boredom with someone else.

BORED INTO ACTION?

*71% of men and 49%
of women said they
fell into and acted on
sexual temptation due
to sexual boredom.*

Angry at my partner

Anger is another tipping point, especially for women. More than a third
(38%) of women said they'd acted on
sexual temptation because they were angry at their partners, compared
to 26% of men. And these numbers cut across all levels of relationship
happiness and sexual satisfaction.

The valuable lesson here is that, if there's a lot of anger in your
relationship, it can be more destructive than you realize. If allowed
to fester, anger grows; and sometimes partners who would otherwise
be faithful are motivated to strike out using sex as their weapon. The
resulting damage may be terminal to the relationship, and yet it can
be avoided by dealing with the anger promptly. So if rage is fueling
your sexual temptation, address the anger before you make matters
much worse than they need to be.

Using social networking sites to flirt, hook up, or cheat

The Normal Bar shows that 55% of women and 42% of men agree
that flirting online is a form of infidelity. When asked if they've ever
done it, only 17% of women and 28% of men said yes, and most of
these players are not happily married or in committed relationships.
So a solid relationship is a strong defense against the temptations of
the Web.

Revenge for my partner's infidelity

We all know that two wrongs don't make a right. Apparently people who've been betrayed know this, too. Only 9% of men and 14% of women said they'd have sex with somebody else as revenge for their partner's infidelity.

High sex drive and "I just can't manage monogamy"

Many people, especially men, who feel they have high needs for sex feel entitled to get their sexual pleasure one way or another. Despite how much or how little they are sexually satisfied in their current relationships, they would cheat and respond, "I just can't help myself." This excuse was the reason 46% of men and 19% of women gave to explain why they'd have sex outside of their relationships. Age, years in relationship, happiness—none of these variables made a difference. There are some people out there who want variety and choose to have sex with other people no matter how sexually satisfied they already are in their relationships. Some people just can't be monogamous, and that's their normal.

Infidelity

Very few people in Western cultures get married with the expectation that they or their partners will have any kind of sexual activity outside their relationships. Marriage vows commonly include "forsaking all others," and while there are a few sexual innovators here and there, the vast majority of men and women believe in monogamy as a personal norm. Indeed, monogamy is so fundamental that most committed couples assume they both agree on it, even if they never discuss it. When the norm of fidelity is violated, partners are first

"Honey, you forgot your lunch this morn—"

shocked and then devastated because they believe the foundation of their marriage and mutual commitment has been shattered.

In other parts of the world, it's assumed that men will cheat, and their wives will have little to say about it. There are a few tribes in Africa and elsewhere that permit women, too, to have sex outside of their main relationship without terrible consequences. There are no large Western, Asian, or Middle Eastern societies that allow women such latitude, however; and most cultures, past and present, do emphasize monogamy between committed partners, even if they don't strictly mandate exclusivity. In some regions, the standard prohibition against extramarital intercourse extends to fantasy, handholding, kissing, and sometimes even staring.

There is one common exception to the rule of monogamy in the

United States: About half of all gay male couples in America allow infidelity based on rules the couple negotiates together. While this is incomprehensible to many people in heterosexual and lesbian relationships, gay men seem to need, want, and be able to tolerate varying degrees of sexual freedom. Research does indicate that gay couples are likely to break up if the outside sex turns into a love affair, but as long as it doesn't, many of these couples seem to be able to maintain long-term, highly committed, and happy relationships without being monogamous.

Other much less common exceptions include heterosexual "swingers" and some smaller groups of people who practice polyandry—having more than two partners who are committed emotionally and sexually to one another. But the overwhelming majority of couples around the world prefer and expect their relationships to be monogamous. Honoring those expectations is another matter.

In your current relationship: Have you been involved with someone else to such an extent that you would consider it an affair?

Our first reaction is that a lot of people will answer this affirmatively. The media paint the picture that affairs are a common occurrence probably because it taps people's fears and gains a wider readership. But maintaining an affair outside your current relationship is not as common as you may think. Only 15% of the people said they've had an affair. This is lower than we expected, which is good, but it's still not great. What differences are there among people whose choose to forget their vows of fidelity?

Of these four broad racial and ethnic categories—Asian, African American, Caucasian, and Hispanic—Asians are notably less likely than the others to cheat. And while our survey data showed that African American couples have one of the highest levels of distrust

In Your Current Relationship: Have You Been
Involved with Someone Else to Such an Extent
That You Would Consider It an Affair?

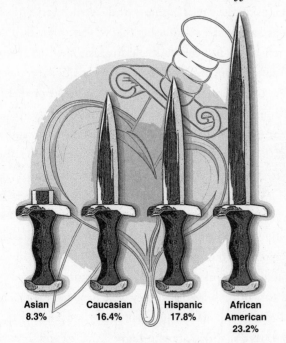

Asian
8.3%

Caucasian
16.4%

Hispanic
17.8%

African
American
23.2%

between partners, their wariness may be warranted given the higher level of infidelity.

Breaking it out by gender, we found large differences. Fourteen percent of women and 26% of men admitted that they'd had an affair. This did not surprise us, given that earlier studies have shown that men have significantly higher rates of infidelity and because of the common notion that women are less likely to be physically or emotionally unfaithful.

Interestingly, this gender difference was not present among respondents under the age of thirty-five. While men (25%) were more likely than women (18%) to admit to having sex outside their current relationship, women (12%) were more likely to say they have had an affair than men (9%). The point is that men are more likely to have sex outside their relationships, while women are more likely to say, they had an outside relationship that was an affair. This new parity may reflect the fact that multiple studies show that the majority of both younger men and women now have multiple partners before marriage, and that multiple partners before marriage predict a higher chance of outside partners within marriage. It is also true that women's rate of infidelity may now match men's simply because women can afford to take care of themselves should the affair be discovered and the relationship dissolved. Women's increasing financial independence gives them the courage and opportunity to explore intimate relationships outside of their main commitment. Then, of course, we have the Internet, which breeds all kinds of unintended liaisons.

We expected to find that people who were happier in their primary relationship would be less likely to have affairs. This is, in fact, the case: 10% of those who said they were happy to extremely happy admitted to an emotional or physical affair, as compared to 24% of those who were slightly happy to slight unhappy and 28% of those who were unhappy or extremely unhappy.

Have you had sex outside your current relationship?

The more disturbing news for most couples is that when the definition of infidelity was broadened from an affair to "having sexual relations outside the primary relationship," the reports of infidelity increased considerably. Now 33% of men and 19% of women admitted to being unfaithful. As for sexual infidelity in the following five ethnic groups, we found that 13% of Asian partners had been sexually active outside their relationship, as had 34% of Mexicans, 24% of other Hispanics, 23% of Caucasians, and 29% of African Americans.

But many of the individuals polled stressed that frequency of sexual infidelity matters. And there is a big difference between a single one-night stand in the course of a twenty-year marriage and a regular pattern of sexual affairs. Seventeen percent of the women who'd been sexually unfaithful and 23% of the men said it happened only once; and 36% of women and 33% of men said it happened two to five times. But that left more than 40% of unfaithful men and women who had to admit that it happened on more of a consistent basis!

The only reassuring news in all this is that sexual satisfaction does afford some protection against infidelity. We found that 46% of men and 35% of women who said they are extremely dissatisfied sexually in their relationships have had sex outside their relationships, compared to just 18% of sexually satisfied men and 14% of satisfied women who've strayed.

It seems that the agreements gay couples make with each other actually cut down on the amount of cheating (if by "cheating" we mean violating a mutual agreement on permissible sexual conduct). They also reduce the likelihood of a true love affair. Just 7% of gay respondents said they've had an affair, which is a vastly lower rate than we found among heterosexual couples. And since affairs are much more likely than random sex to unravel the main relationship, it's just possible that the gay community has something working for their couples that other communities don't. That something may be the ability to be honest about sexual need and temptation. Or it may be that their looser definition of fidelity provides gay couples with some safeguards against serious emotional betrayal.

HONOR YOUR PARTNER

Only 7% of homosexual couples said they'd had an affair during a monogamous relationship.

Does your partner know about the sex you had outside your relationship?

Of those who did have sex outside their relationships, 26% of women and 20% of men told their partners they did it. Another 12% of female partners and 12% of male partners found out on their own. About two-thirds of both women and men (62% and 68% respectively) told us that their partners did not know.

How would you react if you learned your partner had sex outside your relationship?

Men are a lot more forgiving than women when it comes to their partner's potential infidelity. About 44% of men said they'd be disappointed, but would come to terms with it and stay in the relationship. Only one-fourth of all women would do the same. Another 28% of women said they would stay but the relationship would never be the same, and 18% of men agreed. Nearly half (48%) of women and 37% of men said they would feel compelled to dissolve the relationship.

This seems to be the norm in many Western nations. French women, for example, may think their partners are great lovers, but they want them to practice their sexual artistry exclusively at home. Like American women, about half of French women would leave an unfaithful partner. Also as in America, fewer men than women in France would dissolve the relationship solely because of infidelity.

Women may be more conservative about sexual conduct because they are more likely than men to equate sex with emotional connection. About 10% of all men told us they had used a prostitute as a sexual outlet, whereas less than 1% of women said

INTERNATIONAL
CHECKPOINT

44% of women in **France** said they would dissolve the relationship if their partners had sex outside the relationship, compared to 30% of men who said they would call it quits.

they'd ever paid for an equivalent sexual service. The ability of men to compartmentalize sex may make them more tolerant of their partners' unfaithfulness, but they could be mistaken if they think women have extramarital sex for the same reasons they themselves would. For many couples, the repercussions of sexual betrayal can go on for years, if not forever:

"He forgave me (because I sincerely repented with tears) and he never brought it up again. This was 18 years ago." —female, 55, married, with kids

"It's complicated. My spouse doesn't know about, and wouldn't approve of, my opposite-gender extramarital sexual relationships, but is aware of my same-sex relationships." —female, 42, married, with kids

"We're still together but not romantic, and the trust is gone." —male, 54, married, with kids

"We went through counseling, I moved out of the house, we got formally engaged, began going to church together, decided infidelity was totally not acceptable, went through how each of us is responsible for our actions, and how to change those things, and got married a year and a half later." —female, 27, married, no kids

"There are no repercussions. They are all prostitutes, and I just saw them when she was out of town or at work." —male, 63, married, with kids

"He flipped out at first and the first time even called me a whore but he knew that it was a mistake. The second time was actually also considered a mistake but both of these times we did work through it and move on." —female, 18, never married, no kids

"Period of turmoil. Then a truce. I didn't stop." —female, 42, married, no kids

New Normal Advice

Annie and John had been living together for six years when Annie found out that John had cheated on her. She knew the other woman, who was a colleague of John's at work and a friend of both of theirs, so it was a double loss and betrayal. Horrified and humiliated, Annie cried for several sleepless nights and had days when she couldn't work. She wanted to tell John to go to hell. However, as angry as she was, she decided to try to save the relationship.

For some months, Annie and John had been living parallel lives, traveling a lot and barely spending any intimate time together. In fact, they had left the relationship on autopilot, and Annie had to admit that she'd been flirting a bit, too, on the side and had been tempted to get more emotionally involved with someone else herself. So, mindful of her own near trespass, she told John that if he loved her enough to promise never to see the other woman again, they could try to work this out—providing they could find a therapist they both liked, trusted, and respected. John agreed.

John was not proud of his own behavior and he knew the woman he'd been having sex with was not a woman he loved or ever could love. But Annie's reaction surprised him because he'd convinced himself she didn't love him anymore. He felt that having sex with this other woman merely proved his relationship with Annie was over.

In therapy they found out how much they both actually did still love each other but also how afraid each was of not being loved enough. Most of their problems with each another stemmed from this simple but potent fear. After a year in therapy, they worked out their fears and hesitations and made a lifetime commitment to each other. Instead of breaking up, they got married.

Though never welcome, infidelity can present a needed opportunity to make a relationship stronger—if the couple is willing to seek and accept the help of a qualified counselor or therapist. The challenge is to navigate around the barriers of pain and anger, to arrive at a next step that's well thought out and emotionally understood. While working through the facts and emotions surrounding the immediate events, many couples can repair underlying problems and gradually rebuild trust.

TOOL 49 ▶ Head It Off

If you feel attracted to someone other than your partner, avoid the circumstances that increase intimate conversation and contact with this person. As soon as you feel that extra energy, be mindful of it and back away. Most temptations can be handled if you stop them early enough.

TOOL 50 ▶ Share Your Feelings with Your Partner and/or Friends

Do an "end run" around yourself by telling your partner or a close friend that you are feeling attracted to someone else. Enlist others to help dissuade you from acting on your feelings.

By making your temptation "public," you make it much more difficult for yourself to act on it.

Tool 51 ▶ Spend Enough Time Together

The Normal Bar shows that some people are tempted when they feel lonely or angry. One way to reduce those emotions is to put more energy and time into each other. If your partner travels, try to go along at least some of the time. If that's not allowed, make sure there's a legitimate reason! If you are the traveler, try to find a way to take your partner with you now and then. Also, introduce your partner to anyone at work you have a crush on. No secrets!

Tool 52 ▶ Put More Zip in Your Sex Life

While some sexually satisfied people have roving eyes, most stop looking around if sex is exciting and plentiful at home. Try not to get in a rut and if you are in one, get an erotic book, sexy movies, or something sexually titillating to help liven up your sex life. If you're bored, your partner probably is, too, but that can be fixed! A few sessions of love at the beach or on the kitchen table can work wonders.

CHAPTER 14

Addictions, Obsessions, and Bad Behavior

"I'm quitting tomorrow."

When more is not enough, you have a problem, and the *relationship* also has a problem. Too much of anything is a bad idea, no matter what it is. While we may not always be able to stop ourselves from eating, drinking, or smoking too much, when the occasional binge or cigarette turns into a steady pattern of excess, the accumulated damage will take a toll on life balance, health, and family interactions.

Addictive behavior has a biological element. Some people are genetically predisposed to react so strongly to drugs and alcohol, for example, or to the high excitement of gambling or thrill seeking, that the experience of certain behaviors triggers a craving for more. The more the craving is "fed," the stronger it becomes, so that indulgences such as drinking, using, or smoking become habitual. Other psychological factors come into play to make the behavior irresistible; and the addiction, whether to gambling, pornography, alcohol, drugs, or sex with strangers, becomes more important than anything else in the world.

To an addict, not even children, a job, or a loving relationship can compete with the craving. The addiction may produce guilt, self-loathing, loneliness, professional failure, and physical pain and suffering, yet it has such a hold that it overwhelms even abject misery. Partners will try to help. They'll beg, plead, even stage interventions. Such efforts may be successful, but when they're not, the relationship erodes.

If you've never struggled with a real addiction you can count yourself lucky. But even if you aren't personally wrestling with compulsive behavior, you've likely been exposed to someone who is. It's not pretty, and it's a reality that all too many couples have to deal with.

Have you or your partner ever had an addiction while in the relationship?

Women concede they have an addiction less often than men. Just 31% of women admitted to being obsessed or addicted to anything, compared to 39%—approximately one-third of the individuals in our study said they have had at one time or another an addiction or an obsession—of all the men in our study.

Interestingly, this picture changed somewhat when men and women were asked whether their *partners* were addicted. The number of men *reported* to have an addiction by their partners (36%) is about

People Who Said Yes, Their Partners Had an Addiction or an Obsession in the Current Relationship

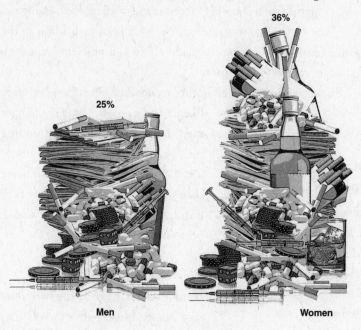

Men   **Women**

on par with the number of men who self-report to having one. However, the percentage of women who were reported by their partners to have a problem (25%) is notably lower than the percentage of women who self-reported.

Of course, each person has his or her own definition of an addiction, and it's possible that men subscribe to a narrower definition. It's also possible that many are in denial. Internationally, the Normal Bar shows that anywhere from 25% to 45% of people believe that their partners have had an addiction. As sociologist W. I. Thomas has observed, what is perceived to be real is real in its consequences. So we decided to dig deeper to find out what people consider to be an addiction and how it affects their relationships.

What are men addicted to?

In no particular order, the Normal Bar shows that porn, alcohol, tobacco, marijuana, technology (Internet use, texting, etc.), eating too much, and playing video games are the addictions men admit to the most. Men also cited verbal/physical abuse as a problem habit with significant relationship impact.

Playing video games and other technology obsessions are more likely to be a problem among younger men, but they also show up among men between the ages of 35 and 45. Older men (45 to 55) are more likely than other age groups to register pornography as an addictive or obsessive behavior.

Men Are Addicted to/Obsessed with:

Porn
Alcohol
Smoking
Marijuana
Eating
Technology
Playing video games

Women Are Addicted to/Obsessed with:

Shopping
Vanity
Alcohol
Smoking
Prescription drugs

What are women addicted to?

In no particular order, the behaviors that women identified as their addictions include obsessive shopping, extreme vanity, alcohol abuse, smoking, and abuse of prescription medications. Women's obsessive behavior was evenly distributed throughout age groups, with the exception of prescription medication abuse, which was most common among women 35 to 44 years of age.

What is the impact of an addiction?

Addiction has a strong reputation for ruining relationships. However, only 18% of women who said they had partners with serious addictions also thought it was ruining their relationships. That said, nearly half (48%) admitted that their partners' problems made their relationships difficult and just over one-third said the problems were not having much of an impact (34%).

A much smaller number of men (6%) said their partners' addictions were ruining their relationships, but more than a third (37%) said their partners' addictions were making their relationships difficult. The majority of men (58%), however, felt that their partners' problems were not having much of an impact. Perhaps there are fewer women with the kinds of addictive or obsessive behaviors that impinge on family or couple life. Or perhaps men are more tolerant than women.

The real surprise is that 28% of those who said they were in a relationship with an addict also said that they were very happy or extremely happy! How can this be?

To begin with, it should be pointed out that among those with a partner who had never had an addiction or an obsession, 52% said they were very happy or extremely happy with their relationship. Clearly, having an addiction or an obsession weighs on a relationship. One additional explanation may be that the addictive behavior in these households had not yet reached the stage of major collateral damage; the addict hadn't yet gotten fired from work, or lost the house, or accumulated massive debt, or become physically or sexually abusive, or abandoned the family. In the early stages of addiction, many addicts can be very persuasive that they have it "under control" or are working on "cleaning up" their act. Another reason could be that the addiction in question involved shopping, vanity, gaming, or another behavior that was obsessive but not as destructive as a major substance abuse problem. At least, it was not perceived to be.

Video games versus smoking

Who would have thought that being addicted to video games could be more detrimental to a relationship than, say, smoking? We all know that smoking kills; and some people are so rabidly against smoking that, at least theoretically, they won't tolerate a smoking partner. On dating sites, one of the most common deal breakers for a prospective date is smoking—when one person smokes and the other doesn't. Still, in our study, smoking didn't seem to have a big impact on couples' happiness or sexual relationship—certainly nothing like the effect of video games! Over half (52%) of the people who said their partners were addicted to video games were also unhappy in the relationship. And why is playing video games for hours on end such a relationship killer? For one thing, the nonplaying partner feels alienated, alone, and rejected. For another, playing video games into the night definitely undermines a couple's sexual intimacy.

Addicted to porn

Research on pornography usually divides the users of pornography and arousing materials into two different groups: those who use porn recreationally and occasionally, and those who are addicted to it as a main source of sexual stimulation. That latter group can be subdivided again between those who are sexually deprived and would turn to a partner if they had one, and those who *prefer* pornography to a real person, including their present partner. There is also a subcategory of people (almost entirely men) who need pornography because they have a fetish that a real partner can't or won't satisfy. This could include a fetish for huge breasts or an extremely large penis, or sadomasochistic acts of a severe nature, or multiple sex partners. But usually when someone complains of a partner's addiction to pornography, the real problem is that the partner prefers pornography over the relationship, or has an insatiable need to view it for hours on end.

In our study, 16% of women said their partners are addicted to porn. How does that affect their relationships? Most (62%) said they are unhappy in their relationships, but the remaining 38% said that despite a partner's addiction to porn, the relationship is happy. Clearly there's a line of fixation that, once crossed, marks trouble for the relationship. A forty-one-year-old woman who left her five-year marriage because of her husband's obsession with online pornography told us what this line looked like to her: "There are lots of signs, and so I got suspicious. I hired a guy who can trace what someone has been looking at on the Internet. What I saw made me feel sick, I was physically ill. I am not going to describe what I saw but there are years of it and it wasn't just naked ladies with big tits and men having sex with them. It was sick and when I confronted him with it, he denied it; and I had the proof!"

However, even a high use of pornography doesn't doom all couples. One woman explained it this way: "We both enjoy pornography. I just wish he didn't use it so much. Occasionally it gets to me because I feel I should be enough for him. But he always reassures me that this is just his fantasy life, and I am his real life, and that the two of them are different. Like when he wants a three-way, he wants to watch his movies (because he knows I'm not going there); but when he wants to make love he only wants me. I asked him once, did he feel like he was missing anything in real life, and I don't know if he was just trying to make me feel better, but he said no."

Another woman, married thirty-two years, put it this way: "I think it's childish and I have told him to hide the stuff so I don't have to look at it. But do I take it personally? No, as long as he doesn't take it personally that I have Johnny Depp in my dreams about once a month!"

What's normal? Most men, especially men with some unsatisfied desires, will use pornography. This is true whether they are straight or gay. Gay partners, who often watch it themselves, understand that it's not necessarily a comment on the relationship. Most women in heterosexual couples, unless they are watching it, too, tend to resent it, but it's only when the habit becomes an obsession, and when the content is disturbing, that the issue becomes a threat to the relationship.

Is your partner trying to eliminate the addiction?

Addictions are notoriously difficult to break, and true addicts will do almost anything to avoid having their drug supply (be that cigarettes or five-martini lunches) withdrawn. Tellingly, only half of men and women with an addicted partner said the partner is trying to quit. This creates an impossible situation for these spouses—unless they are codependent (aiding and abetting the addiction in some way) or addicted themselves. Those who neither support nor share the addiction must watch helplessly as their partners go downhill and potentially unravel the relationship and economic welfare of the household. There are support groups (both Alcoholics Anonymous and Narcotics Anonymous offer family support meetings and counseling), but that doesn't erase all the pain, disappointment, and financial and emotional vulnerability that addictions cause.

When we asked people to tell us more about how they handle their partner's habits and the consequences of the addiction, we received a staggering number of stories about alcohol abuse, physical/verbal abuse, and cigarette, drug, and pornography addictions. Most were in the context of ongoing addictions. Many partners said they'd kept the problem secret and didn't know where to turn for help in breaking the cycle. Others had been trying to do something for a while and were very frustrated. Still others ended with triumph over the addiction, but one unfortunate common denominator in these stories was that the turning point for the addicts usually depended on a dire threat—the realization that their partners were leaving, or that they were going to lose their families, or that they had almost died. Several people mentioned that twelve-step programs or other counseling helped them transition back into a healthier lifestyle.

"My husband has been trying to control his pornography choices. I do not mind him watching pornography; however, there are a few genres of adult entertainment that I take issue with that he has a taste for. He usually goes a few months, then relapses into it. His addiction to war gaming isn't, and never will be, fixed, despite my pleadings." —female, 21, married 3 years

"We are both potheads and we've occasionally pushed each other while fighting." —male, 31, in a 3-year committed relationship

"My partner is still dealing with alcohol issues related to undiagnosed depression and self-medication. He cannot seek medical help due to unemployment and lack of insurance and stupid macho pride. Ongoing issue that is threatening the security of our relationship." —female, 32, in a 3-year committed relationship

"I have experienced some physical violence. However, I experience daily verbal, emotional, and psychological abuse. We've been in marriage counseling off and on for the entire marriage. The abuse has not been resolved. It is just taking different forms." —female, 40, married 10 years, with kids

"The only addiction was mine—I smoked for 25 years. I chose to quit cold turkey January 1 and haven't looked back. If I'm being honest, I did it for my partner more than anything—she hated I did it. It's one of my life's best decisions." —male, 52, married 7 years

"I married a very insecure person. He has alienated practically everyone, including family, at one time or another. Knows he is bipolar; won't do anything about it. He has been to anger management and played it to the end. I have been pushed, shoved, choked, and verbally abused. Counseling has helped me deal with it better than I used to." —female, 53, married 20 years, with kids

"She abuses me physically and verbally at the same time, whenever she accuses me of cheating. Problem still continues to date." —male, 37, married 6 years

"His addiction to drugs destroyed our family. He was so angry and high on who knows what one day that he took an ax to our wooden bed frame and chopped it up because he said I complained about it one too many times." —female, 26, married 4 years, with kids

Antidepressants, violence, and psychological problems

Use of SSRI (selective serotonin reuptake inhibitor) medications, or antidepressants such as Prozac and Zoloft, has become so widespread in the United States and elsewhere that nearly a quarter (23%) of our respondents told us they are currently taking some form of these prescription drugs. People take them for everything from anger and paranoia to anxiety, as well as for clinical depression. We've even heard of them being prescribed for impotence!

We wondered what effect, if any, the use of these medications has on relationships. One clue was the difference between how many people are actually taking them and how many of their partners *know* they're taking them. The number is about par for women—24% are taking them and 23% of men know about it. But while 22% of men told us they take antidepressants, only 11% of women know that their partners are taking them.

There is still an unfortunate stigma around mental illness that makes it difficult for some people to admit—even to their partners—that they need medication. The truth, however, is that these drugs normally have a positive impact on people's well-being and relationships. The Normal Bar showed that a large majority (62%) of people taking them also said they are happy to extremely happy in their relationships, essentially the same percentage as those not taking such medications. The one downside is sexual, since most antidepressants lower libido in both men and women and may make it more difficult to climax. So, it's no surprise that 28% of those taking such medication said they were satisfied or very satisfied with their sex life, as compared to 39% of those who were not.

Verbal and physical abuse

Loving couples are normally gentle with each other. However, 21% of women and 17% of men told us that they have been violently pushed, shoved, hit, or threatened in their relationships. These statistics may make women almost as aggressive as men, but they don't reflect equal combat. While women do push and shove and can be abusive, research shows that men's larger size and strength makes their violence more physically destructive. Men typically land far more punishing blows and inflict most of the serious injuries in abusive relationships. Likewise, among same-sex couples, violence between male gay partners is much more dangerous than what takes place between lesbians.

This kind of punishing and destructive behavior unfortunately occurs in all kinds of families and at all ages. But the risk of violence does seem to rise the longer a couple has been together. About 7% of partners in a relationship of one year or less said they've experienced abusive behavior, but 30% of those who've been together a decade or more said they have been abused.

This is a special area of relationship trauma. It's not exactly right to classify it as an addiction, but unfortunately, people who use vicious words and name-calling, or who push, shove, punch, or worse, rarely engage in these behaviors just once. There is no doubt that if verbal and physical abuse is your norm, it will ultimately do serious damage, even if the relationship doesn't break up. People stay in abusive relationships for many reasons and sometimes become so acclimated to violence that they think it's normal. Women, in particular, often stay because they think they have no place else to go, or because they're terrified of worse abuse—even death—if they try to leave.

Violence in a relationship is *not* normal. In fact, it is pathological and often is related to serious addiction. When drugs or alcohol fogs one partner's capacity for understanding, ignites bursts of rage and violence, and kills the desire to protect and love, then there's no positive energy or focus left for the relationship. The answer does not lie in the healthy partner's reactions but in professional therapy, counseling, and recovery. If you are reading this and you know that you or your partner has significant problems with substance abuse, anger, or violence, then gather up your courage and get the professional help you need to set your life—and your relationship—back on track.

Is your partner controlling?

There is one other abnormal type of relationship abuse that sometimes slips under the radar. No punches are thrown, no shoves completed, but one partner nevertheless controls and intimidates the other to the point that the controlled partner is unable to function freely as an adult. This creates misery for the oppressed partner; of the 8% of men and women who told us that their partners are extremely controlling, 83% said they are very unhappy in their relationships.

The irony is that very controlling people are usually insecure. They try to dominate their partners because they're afraid that otherwise something will happen to make them feel jealous or wronged. This kind of domination is insulting, frightening, and, to say the least, unlikely to motivate love or trust.

When counseling should be part of your normal

Problems such as addiction, rage, violence, and mental illness aren't part of most couples' normal, and shouldn't be anyone's. Fortunately, with the right kind of professional help, even seriously troubled individuals can be reborn and relationships revived.

The challenge is to find the therapist or counselor who is best equipped to help you with your particular problems. It's also critical that both partners be open to the process and willing to make an honest effort. Unfortunately, not enough people try or keep trying until they find the right therapist for them. If you decide to consult a therapist, get referrals from people whose judgment you trust, and have a preliminary meeting to get a feel for the therapist before you commit to going forward with that person. If one or both partners feel it's not a good fit, move on to another referral.

New Normal Advice

Doreen was married for five years to Jake, an alcoholic and a drug addict who verbally abused her. They had two kids together, and almost every interaction any family member had with Jake was traumatic. His norm was to control Doreen with a torrent of criticism. Neither she nor the kids could do anything right in his eyes. She walked on eggshells trying to stay safe and keep her kids out of harm's way because she never knew what was in store when Jake was around.

Doreen repeatedly broke up with Jake, then, time and time again, moved back in with him. Her friends could not understand how she would expose her daughters to Jake, much less herself, but Doreen had a million excuses to justify this pattern. Actually, she had a history of being with men like Jake. It was as if she herself was addicted—to abusive partners.

It took Jake's coming home drunk and threatening to kill her and the kids for Doreen finally to leave him. The night that happened, she called the police. While they took Jake to jail and booked him, Doreen grabbed the kids and moved out. To save her liberty and her sanity, she moved to a different city, got a different job, and tried to make a new start.

Unfortunately, Jake represented Doreen's normal, and she didn't know how to create a better one. She was unfamiliar with loving, kind relationships. Soon Doreen met Roland, another alcoholic, at a bar. Even though Roland was a major consumer of pornography as well as alcohol, she moved herself and her two girls in with him. She was with him for years, always trying to get him to stop drinking, always failing.

When Doreen finally left Roland—and went back to Jake—her friends decided enough was enough. For years they'd challenged Doreen's decisions, but even when she ignored them, they would stand by her side. Now several of her friends staged an intervention. They confronted Doreen with the fact that she was as addicted to self-destructive relationships as the people she chose were addicted to alcohol, porn, or drugs.

Doreen's self-esteem was low, but her friends reminded her how special she was, that she deserved a healthy relationship and must not settle for anything less. Her friends stood by her, checking in daily and helping her move away from Jake and Roland. Doreen needed a lot of support but she listened to her friends and now steers clear of any men who show signs of unhealthy addictions.

It's easy to get drawn into repetitive self-destructive habits and self-destructive people. There may be some good times in between bouts of addictive behavior, but those scattered good times are a poor substitute for reliable love, kindness, loyalty, respect, and self-respect. If you or your partner has an addiction or pattern of violent behavior that seems unbreakable, you need to commit wholeheartedly to changing your normal and to get whatever help you need to succeed.

TOOL 53 ▶ Give Friends Veto Power

Are you the nonaddict who seems to continually pick partners who have significant problems? If so, don't let yourself choose the next significant person in your life. Admit that you have bad selection antenna and entrust the choice of your dates to close friends who have proven to have better judgment. If you're considering a new partner—or returning to the old one—consult these friends first and take their advice. They can help you identify the warning signs you need to avoid as well as your own dangerous vulnerabilities. With their guidance, you may learn to love qualities in people you never even noticed before.

TOOL 54 ▶ Get Some Self-Esteem in Class

It may sound odd, but one of the major reasons people put up with addicted partners (or have problems themselves) is that they are imbued with a deep sense of unworthiness. This can be fixed! Look on the Web for classes in self-esteem near you. If you don't think much of yourself, that's the first thing you've got to change in order to create a new normal.

TOOL 55 ► Change Your Addictive Nature into a Good Addiction

Psychologists describe what is called an addictive personality. Let's say this applies to at least some addicts. One strategy, then, is to replace the destructive addiction with a new, *constructive* addiction. For example, instead of heading to the bar each evening, go to the gym. Instead of wallowing in smoke and drink, spend those hours after work buffing up for a state weight-lifting or body-sculpting contest. Take that extreme part of yourself and put it to use where it will do some good.

TOOL 56 ► Change Your Friends and Change Your Address

Sometimes your friends feed your problem. If your social life is all about drinking, make the effort to develop a new network based on healthier activities and interests such as hiking, rock climbing, books, or the arts. Get out of your old habits and into new ones that don't place temptation in your path. Choose friends who support, encourage, and are happy to keep you company in your new normal.

CHAPTER 15

Commitment—Should I Stay or Should I Go?

"Herbert! What took you so long? You know how much
I hate waiting."
"Is it too late for me to take the hell option?"

If you knew you'd spend an eternal afterlife with your partner, would you grin or would you groan? Of course, this question takes the vow "Till death do us part" to a whole new level, but people's answers are still revealing. Four-fifths of women we asked and nearly three-fourths of men said they'd be thrilled to spend eternity with their current partners! And, surprisingly, the duration of the relationship

57% of men and women who are unhappy *in their relationships said they would still be happy to be with their mates in the afterlife!*

made little difference in their answers. Couples in their twenty-first year in love were as likely to relish an eternity together as honeymooners.

The stunning news, however, is that nearly 60% of both men and women who are *unhappy* with their relationships said they would *still* be happy to spend eternity with their mates! Security and familiarity are powerful bonds, perhaps even powerful enough to trump unhappiness. Still, the prospect of "forever after" with a mate who makes you miserable is not a cheery thought. There must be a better option.

How Committed Are You?

The thought of spending the rest of your life with one person could be simultaneously comforting and daunting. It's comforting to be able to construct a set of life goals and mutual hopes, to believe that the two of you are going to help each other through life. At the same time, the enormity of this commitment can be intimidating. And that's true at any age! It's not easy to imagine one's whole life cycle, much less a partnership that will last for life. No one knows at the outset what will be required, and as partners grow and change it can be a challenge to grow together. All long-term relationships have their ups and downs, and the willingness to navigate and negotiate these changes is a vital part of commitment.

We wondered how commitment normally weathers over time, and if our couples could divulge any secrets to long-term happiness.

Would you put your life on the line to save your partner?
Several years ago a couple was biking in one of the national parks when a cougar attacked the man and brought him down. His female partner jumped off her bike and beat the cougar off by slamming it with the bicycle until it ran off. Then, although her partner was gravely injured, she loaded him onto her bike and carried him back to civilization, doctors, and survival. She put her own life on the line for his.

There's no stronger or more moving act of commitment than to risk your own life to save your partner's. So we asked: "Imagine a situation where you'd have to possibly sacrifice your own life to save your partner's life; would you?" We learned that 78% of women and 93% of men said they would risk their life to save their partners. A noble norm!

What might account for the difference between men and women? Perhaps the higher number of would-be male heroes reflects a vestige of chivalry, or perhaps the drive to protect is just hardwired into the male of the species. It could also be that women hesitate out of concern for dependents, especially young children, who would be orphaned if their heroic effort failed and both parents died. Or perhaps some women's confidence in their lifesaving skills and strength was such that they felt it would be suicidal to even try.

There are some other important differences. The Normal Bar results shifted when we factored in the happiness of the relationship. Predictably, extremely unhappy women are much less likely to put their lives in danger to save a partner. A full third of them flatly said they would refuse. However, just as many men who are extremely unhappy in their relationships as men in happy couples—93%—would *still* risk their lives to save their partners! There's been a lot of research on men's more "macho" side, and the urge to be a hero is widespread among males. Young men throughout history have gone off to war to protect people they do not know and might not even like if they were to meet, so the idea of honor may be more important to men than their affection for the person they're saving.

True Heroes?

93% of men said they would risk their lives to save a partner, even in a bad *relationship!*

Would your partner put his or her life on the line to save you?
The Normal Bar data showed that most people would risk their lives for their partners; but do they trust that their partners would save them? While the norm still shows a high level of trust, the numbers suggest that people have substantially less confidence in their

partners' than in their own valor. Just 72% of men and 79% of women thought their partners would risk their lives for them, which shows that about one-fourth of all people doubt that their partners would save them in a crisis.

But maybe these numbers reflect honest assessments of ability rather than emotional commitment? The Normal Bar suggests otherwise. When we looked at only the responses from couples with an extremely strong sexual connection, we found that 87% of both men and women believe their partners would jump in front of a speeding car to save their lives. Connection breeds confidence between partners.

Would you choose your current relationship again?

Just for a moment, let's pretend you're single. . . . Would you choose to start over with your current partner, or would you choose a different person and relationship? You might be surprised to learn that the norm is to stay true! Over three-quarters of the people in this study (78% of women and 73% of men) said they're committed to the same person and relationship. Most couples do not regret being together, nor are they pining for "the one that got away." This speaks very well for most people's ability to choose their partners well.

Nevertheless, changing circumstances can impact commitment. We did see a big dive to 54% when we asked those who are extremely unhappy in the overall relationship and sexually dissatisfied if they'd do it again—but that's *still* more than half who would stay put. So what is keeping those extremely unhappy people tethered to their mates? It's not their children. According to our data, unhappy people who have kids are no more or less committed to their partners than those who don't. The culprits may be hope and love, which spring eternal even when couples are unhappy and frustrated. With insights from the Normal Bar, perhaps some of these troubled but romantic couples can move into a new normal that restores the relationships they so value.

Does your partner love you more now, or less?

Love normally endures! When we looked closely at our happiest couples, we found that 70% believed their partners love them more now than when they first met, and another 25% believe that their level of love is the same.

But among those who aren't feeling as loved and happy, there's a worrisome gender difference. More than a quarter (28%) of men said they feel less loved than when their relationships were new, compared to just 17% of women. We don't know if they actually are loved less, but for those who only think they're less cherished the pain is just as real.

Assuming the love actually is still there, much of this pain could be avoided with some of the simple tools we've offered in this book. People need affection, affirmation, and reassurance, and when they don't feel that forthcoming, their relationships suffer.

Just showing affection in a small way or saying "I love you" often changes the tenor and emotional temperature. If you are reading this and do love your partner, ask if he or she feels more, less, or the same amount of love since you first fell in love. If this question scares you, there's a good chance your relationship requires more expressions of love.

Should I Stay or Should I Go?

When love does not endure, the inevitable question arises: Is it time to break up? In the United States the divorce rate tells us that about 50% of all married couples at some point do untie the knot. But as anyone who's ever done it knows, breaking up really is hard to do, which is why so many people lie, cheat, and suffer to avoid it. The Normal Bar confirms this, showing that a quarter of partners are anywhere from *unhappy to extremely unhappy* in their relationships, yet they continue year after year, telling themselves, "This is as good as I'm going to get," or "This is just the way it is." These people may be unhappier than they need to be, since even a devitalized or disappointing relationship can be made better—a lot better.

Happiness is not just a matter of luck. It requires desire and careful tending. The Normal Bar shows that happy couples nurture each other, communicate well, and maintain emotional and sexual intimacy. Sure, there are times when relationships are hard work, but that "work" pays off! Even the smallest of acts and words that foster and maintain intimacy can turn a relationship around. But *both* partners need to want to create or restore happiness and be willing to redirect their time and energy toward pleasing and understanding each other. When one or both partners refuse to participate in this revitalization process, breaking up may seem like the only way to create a new and better normal.

Who contemplates breaking up more, men or women?

It's normal to think about breaking up. There's no differentiation between the sexes here: Men and women are equally matched when it comes to considering other options. More than a third (37%) say they think about breaking up *all the time* or *often,* and another 33% say they *sometimes* think about it. Only 12% say they never think about it and 20% say they rarely do.

Not surprisingly, the number is much higher among unhappy couples, where 87% of partners contemplate leaving their relationships. But even 34% of extremely happy partners think about breaking up from time to time. Normal relationships ebb and flow!

"Should I stay or should I go?"

***Have the media affected your feelings about your relationship
to the point where you thought more seriously about leaving?***
The media are more powerful than they deserve to be. They shape
our reactions to ourselves, to products, to love, sex, and relationships.
Even though most of us know that mass media often misrepresent
normalcy in relationships, we are nonetheless affected by what we see
and hear. The media glorify romance and give us the happy endings
we want in romantic comedies, while also overdramatizing negative
relationships. If you believed what you saw on television and in the
movies, you'd think every third woman was in danger of being mur-
dered by her boyfriend or husband, that people fall in love at first sight

and end up together because of fate, and that one partner in every couple is about to be seduced by the family's best friend. Even so-called *reality* shows intentionally distort reality by concentrating either on truly dysfunctional couples or on impossibly glamorous ones. Ultimately, if we believe what we see, our own daily decisions also will be distorted, perhaps because we want what the media tell us other people have (though they don't) or

FATAL DISTRACTIONS

Over one-third of men and women can remember watching a TV show or movie that affected them so much they considered breaking up!

because, by comparison with the truly disastrous and bizarre relationships on TV, our own lives seem healthier than they really are. Real problems often aren't as dramatic as those we see on the screen, but that doesn't mean we can afford to ignore them.

Given the plentiful research on the impact of media on human relationships, we decided to ask if this influence went so far as to prompt serious thoughts about breaking up. More than a third—37% of females and 36% of males—said it had! This is alarming. When people base major real-life decisions on the illusions of love presented by larger-than-life screen romances, terrible mistakes can be made. No one's relationship can measure up to the mega-moments of love, sex, and excitement that Hollywood generates—especially not all the time.

If you have contemplated leaving your partner, what scares you most?

The number-one thing that scares men and women about leaving their partners is the possibility that they'd *regret* it. When asked what most held them back, 37% of women and 27% of men said they're afraid of living with a lifetime of regret. These people understand that no one can predict the future, and in most cases, a decision to leave cannot be undone.

The second most common breakup fear is of hurting the other partner. This was the reason 18% of men and 12% of women gave for being afraid to leave.

The third scariest thing about leaving is the prospect of being alone. This was the specter named by 11% of men and 14% of women.

Surprisingly, kids and money did not rank in the top three choices of separation anxieties. Money may be less of an issue since so many women now earn enough to support themselves, but the lack of concern about children is surprising given the stereotype—often backed up by historical practice—of couples "staying together for the sake of the children." Perhaps the norm is shifting as people conclude that their own happiness is more in their children's best interests than staying in a troubled and unsatisfying marriage.

Social scientists recently have battled over the impact of divorce on children's well-being. Respected researchers like Mavis Hetherington have found that leaving a conflict-ridden marriage is better for children, while others, such as Linda Waite, argue the contrary. All these experts worry about the impact on children if divorce leaves the household a great deal poorer, and the age of the children seems to make a significant difference. For example, during a child's early years, most mothers have less ability to go out and work to become economically viable. Likewise, adolescence is often turbulent enough for kids that some parents won't want to add a divorce to their teenagers' emotional burden. But there seems to be as much or more popular sentiment in favor of leaving for the good of the children as there is for staying in a rotten marriage because of the kids.

Unfortunately, not everyone is rational about deciding when enough is enough.

What causes the most stress in your relationship?

Ours may be the first generation to know exactly how toxic and dangerous stress really is. Most of us are aware that stressful situations are harmful to our bodies, minds, and relationships. It's not good for anyone to come home after a particularly stressful day at work and meet a bombardment of crisis, anger, accusations, misery, and general negativity. A recurring pattern like this will take its toll on every member of the household. Stress ultimately is what tips couples over the edge to break up.

While money and lifestyle issues and raising kids are all important, when we asked people to name the main causes of stress in their

Main Causes of Stress in a Relationship

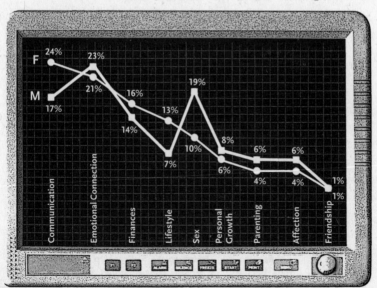

relationships, 24% of women said communication and 23% of men said emotional connection.

To reduce stress, then, couples need to be able to talk things over and ramp up their emotional and sexual intimacy. Having a sense of close connection is the buffer that allows partners to weather the blows of life as well as the misunderstandings and disappointments that inevitably appear in long-term relationships. Without these two sources of strength, stress levels can go through the roof, endangering the health of each partner, and the health of the relationship and family.

Do you ever consider breaking up?

Given that sometimes it's sheer commitment alone that gets people through an unhappy period and into a happy one, we asked people: *Thinking about your current relationship, do you think it is likely that you'll stay together forever or break up?* A solid 71% of men and 72% of women told us they'd never break up with their current partners. However, for almost a third of our respondents, the prospects are not so rosy. A sizable minority seems to be "sticking it out" for just the

Level of Commitment

FEMALE   MALE

5%   5%   8%   8%   11%   10%   5%   5%

Break up within the next few months   **Break up within the year**   **Break up within 5 years**   **Break up within 10 years**

next five or ten years, and about 30% in all *expect* to break up. And that's just people who *know* that their relationships are shaky or about to be over. Some people who answered "forever" may have a partner who's looking for an exit.

When do you know it's time to break up?

Thinking of leaving is one thing, but telling your partner it's over is another. If the relationship is emotionally or physically violent, leaving may be decided by one screaming fight or slamming door too many. If it's a relationship that is limping along, however, and only one person is truly miserable enough to want out, the last straw can be difficult to identify, much less explain. This is why people may know that the love is gone for years without even broaching the subject of leaving.

While breakups can appear sudden and inexplicable to outsiders, the Normal Bar data show that most people in terminal relationships torture themselves about leaving, and stay together a lot longer than they should. Even when one is sure that leaving is the right thing to do, it still takes fortitude, and sometimes courage,

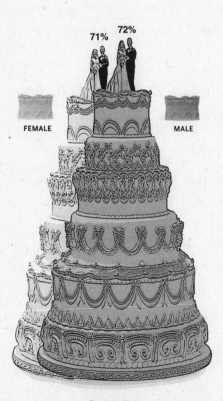

71%   72%

FEMALE   MALE

Be together
forever

THE TIPPING POINT

You'll know you're ready to leave the relationship when it's easier to go than to stay.

to do the deed. For the person who is being left, reactions may vary from relief to immeasurable pain. For all involved, the consequences are grave enough that the person leaving needs to be sure the relationship truly is over. One key signal is the realization that leaving is easier than staying. Here are some others:

"I left my husband after he tried to throw me out of a moving car when we were in a big fight." —female, 41, married 11 years, with kids

"When she told me that she thought there was somebody better out there for her. As soon as I heard that, I was done." —male, 44, married 15 years, with kids

"I left him because I noticed that he doesn't love me anymore." —female, 34, in a 6-year committed relationship

"She had an online relationship with somebody she never met for over a year, and I couldn't bring myself to trust her again." —male, 38, married 6 years

"I knew I was done when my husband drove with our kids in the car while he was drunk." —female, 43, married 16 years

Have you ever had relationship counseling with a professional (such as a psychologist, marriage therapist, etc.)?

When people are in a troubled relationship (or one that has gone through a period of being troubled) many reach out for professional help. We wanted to know how many of our couples have seen a counselor and, if they have, if it made a difference in the outcome. More than a third (39%) of people in our study said they've had relationship counseling. Unfortunately, their feedback on this professional help mirrors the findings of renowned clinical researcher Neil Jacobson, who found that counseling is a mixed bag. More than half (54%) of people who sought counseling say it didn't change their relationships, 39% said it helped, and another 7% said it actually made things worse.

The reality is that not all counselors are equally gifted or trained to deal with every situation. It's critical to seek out a professional who is well qualified to treat the specific problems occurring in your relationship. It also helps to see a therapist early in the game, instead of waiting until the issues are irresolvable. All relationships go through demanding and difficult periods, and when the going gets truly rough, the insights and support of a trained professional can make all the difference. Some people, unfortunately, treat therapy as an exit strategy and never give it a chance.

New Normal Advice

Vincent and Rosalie had been married for twenty-five years, only the first few of which were idyllic. Rosalie was a busy and successful career woman with exacting standards—standards she extended to Vincent. He tried hard to please her but knew he was failing to live up to her expectations. For example, she felt sex should be passionate and innovative every single time. She felt Vincent should earn as much as she did and often chided him for not reaching his full potential. She was also annoyed that he wasn't as physically fit as she was. This constant barrage of judgment made Vincent defensive and so angry that he sometimes got verbally abusive, threw things, and threatened to leave. A few days later he'd apologize, but Rosalie carried a grudge. It could take a very long time for them to make up, and even when they did get back to "normal," it wasn't long before they blew up all over again.

Finally Rosalie said, "If you talk to me like that again, I'm leaving." This tempered Vincent for a while, but just recognizing his anger management problem was not enough to solve it, much less the other underlying problems. The next time he felt criticized and exploded, Rosalie moved out. She stayed at her brother's house for a week before she would even answer Vincent's phone calls. She wouldn't have talked to him at all if not for their two children, who were in high school.

They both knew the relationship was in jeopardy. They'd spent more than two decades together, but that wasn't reason enough to stay married. In fact, they each had been seeing therapists separately who recommended divorce. Finally, as a last gasp, they agreed to try couples therapy.

The new therapist persuaded Rosalie and Vincent to reexamine the ways that each of them ignited the other's anger and pain. Once they understood how they were undermining each other's egos, they could change their behavior and start to mend the emotional safety net that currently was in tatters. They still had a chance to retrieve very valuable parts of their marriage.

With the help of therapy, Vincent realized how much of his anger mismanagement he'd learned in childhood. Rosalie realized how cruel she had unintentionally been to Vincent. They learned to give each other "warning words" when either one of them went into the behavior that had put them on the brink of divorce. They also started going out on dates, doing more pleasurable things together, and recovering the sense of fun they'd enjoyed early in their relationship. This helped them fall in love again. When Vincent didn't feel disrespected, and when Rosalie felt heard, when they stopped undermining the love and safety of their marriage, their mutual commitment to each other and to the relationship was renewed.

Tool 57 ▶ Help Your Partner Feel More Secure

Even long-term, seemingly confident partners can feel insecure about how much they are loved. The slightest feelings of insecurity can destabilize an otherwise healthy relationship. People start to run for cover if they think they're unappreciated, unnecessary, or unwanted. When partners feel unloved or just one bad argument away from a breakup, they might start looking for someone who doesn't make them feel so marginalized.

So, practice giving some kind of reassurance every day. Do small but significant acts that show commitment. Make affectionate jokes about what it's like to know you are together forever, and let your partner know that his or her call is always welcome, no matter what time or place.

Always be in the moment! When you are with your partner, *be there*, mentally and physically. This sounds so simple, but not many people do it. Soothe insecurities with kindness and love, instead of getting angry, snarky, or defensive. If you can help your partner feel more relaxed and secure, you'll receive a lot more help making the relationship hum.

Tool 58 ▶ Make a *Bigger* Commitment Gesture Every So Often

Talk is good, but actions are better. A big gesture that demonstrates love and commitment is worth many verbal reassurances. Throw a surprise birthday party or make a video showing your relationship from its very beginnings. Plan the trip your partner has always wanted and make it a surprise. Create a scrapbook of your partner's life, or enroll in a course together that is central to your partner's interests. You'll be rewarded not only with gratitude but also with an intensification of love.

Tool 59 ▶ If Commitment Is an Issue—See a Professional

If you see continuing signs of real discontent in your relationship, start looking for help. If your partner declines to plan for the future or invest in enough couple time, or if you both seem significantly less engaged with each other than you used to be, it's more than time for professional advice and guidance. If you feel the love is declining, or in any way feel weaker rather than stronger as a couple, don't wait until the relationship is beyond resuscitation. Even if you still feel good about the relationship, just not as good as you used to feel, think about going to a marriage enrichment seminar or couples workshop. Almost every church or religious group offers programs to make couples' relationships better, and many independent psychologists and therapists have getaways that are fun as well as reconstructive. We offer some great book recommendations in the resource section at the end of this book.

CHAPTER 16

The Pursuit of
Relationship Happiness

"See, honey? I told you we could be even happier!
It really does exist."

Having a fulfilling relationship isn't like winning the lottery. In the relationship sweepstakes, the odds are not just in your favor; they're under your control! You choose the normal you live. Whether it's a happy or unhappy normal is entirely up to you.

The encouraging truth, as the Normal Bar shows, is that most people have found ways to be happy together, and it's not that hard to fix an ailing relationship. When we asked people to rate their level of happiness within their relationships, 74% said they are happy! These results tell us that it's *normal* for couples to be happy. What's more, it's normal for men and women to be equally happy. We found that 14% of women and 14% of men consider themselves extremely happy; 26% of women and 25% of men say they are very happy; and another 34% of women and 35% of men say they are relatively happy in their relationships.

Why, then, do we hear so much about the 26% of couples who are unhappy? There's no shortage of stories in the news, in other media, or among friends about spousal abuse, cheating, or divorce. When's the last time you read a story about happy couples making their relationships even better? We too rarely pay attention to couples who have fun and laugh together, who tell each other how much they love each other, and who find new ways to keep the flame of sexual interest alight. The reality is that problems make better stories, in part because we're wired to focus on conflict and in part because we enjoy the illusion that we can fix problems—even if they're problems in a story about strangers.

TRUE NORMAL

Being happy *in a relationship.*

Also, there's a widespread notion that we can't fix what's not broken, so happy relationships slide under our radar, leaving our antennae tuned for signals of trouble. The real problem is that if we pay attention only to the negative, we tend to neglect the positive normalcy of our own relationship.

We asked people to select the source of their greatest level of personal happiness from seven different options—or from an "other" option if we didn't list their choice. A loving relationship was chosen as the most important contributor to happiness in every single country in our study! Money and professional success did not even come close.

More than half of both women (54%) and men (56%) said their happiness depends on their relationships. A distant second most popular source of happiness is children (for 12% of women and 9% of men). Health comes in third, for 7% of the females and 10% of the males.

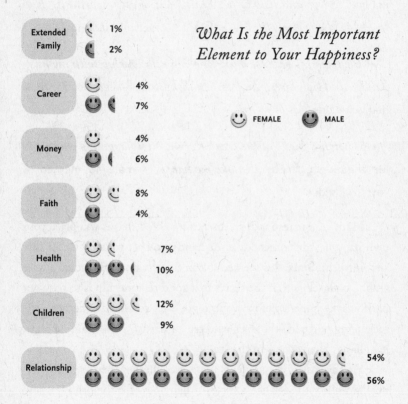

What Is the Most Important Element to Your Happiness?

Extended Family — 1% / 2%

Career — 4% / 7%

Money — 4% / 6%

Faith — 8% / 4%

Health — 7% / 10%

Children — 12% / 9%

Relationship — 54% / 56%

FEMALE   MALE

Here are some of our respondents' comments about happiness:

"As I've gotten older, I've developed a stronger sense of self; I've learned that happiness doesn't come from things or conditions, really, but from within." —female, 48, never married, no kids

"My sense of being in control of my own life is probably the number-one factor in my happiness." —female, 27, never married, no kids

"I feel that the life lessons my boyfriend has taught me are almost completely responsible for how happy I have become. He has taught me how to love and how to feel again. But, most importantly, how to feel good about myself." —female, 18, never married, no kids

"I'm the happiest because of my ongoing relationship with my husband, our 13 children, and 19 grandchildren." —female, 71, married, with kids

"Just knowing that I'm the creator of my own happiness empowers me to do what it takes to make me happy." —male, 48, married 18 years, with kids

Many of our respondents also commented that if you place your own happiness in somebody else's hands, you set yourself up for disappointment. Since this seemed to run counter to conventional advice among counselors that the secret to a good relationship is to put your partner's happiness before your own, we wondered whether self-sacrificing partners, the ones who try hardest to please, are more, or less, happy than others in the study.

First we asked respondents to decide whether they or their partners are likely to sacrifice their own happiness for the other person. The Normal Bar shows that men and women both are willing to put their own happiness aside for the greater good when they have kids. But if children are removed from consideration, 73% of women said they'd put their own happiness ahead of their partners'. A comparatively smaller number of childless men, 54%, said they'd look out for themselves first. But that's still more than half who are me-firsters.

When we compared people's levels of happiness, we discovered that most people who said they look out primarily for themselves eventually have problems in their relationships. But we also found that extreme self-sacrifice is a no-win strategy. If you look out only for your partner and never for yourself, this causes as much lopsidedness as having a partner who's just in it for him- or herself.

The happiest couples told us that each partner personally prevails in making important decisions about half of the time. These couples also said they work hard to find a mutually happy outcome, and compromise when necessary. This seems to be the core secret for relationship happiness: frequent compromises over time, and balance in giving and getting, conceding and winning. Read this as a Big Message if you've been trying to keep the peace in the relationship by saying yes to everything.

TOP PRIORITY

Taking kids out of the equation, 73% of women said they put their own happiness first!

How do we envision a happy normal relationship? To find out if the general concept of a "normal relationship" is changing, we came up with six normal categories, asked our respondents which category best described their own attitudes toward their relationships right now, then analyzed which category has the highest correlation with overall happiness and sexual satisfaction.

The six "normal" categories are:

TRADITIONAL: A person who still subscribes to the traditional values of commitment and unconditional love.

DREAMER: A person who visualizes what a relationship should be like with an ideal person whom they've created in their mind. Dreamers tend to find faults when they meet or date people who don't fit their ideal image.

INDEPENDENT: A person who has his or her own agenda at times and is very comfortable being single. Independents don't feel their mission in life is to find somebody to take care of them, but they definitely welcome good company.

UNDECIDED: A person who isn't quite sure what he or she wants from one day to the next. At times the Undecideds know exactly what they want and feel, but then just as quickly as that feeling arrives, it can shift to something completely different.

SELF-SACRIFICER: A person who tends to put every available ounce of energy into the relationship. Self-sacrificers hold themselves to a high standard of caretaking and sometimes they're totally unselfish; but, other times, they resent being the major or only "giver." If Self-sacrificers commit to a manipulative or ungrateful partner, they end up in a very unhealthy relationship.

ALTERNATIVE: A person who doesn't let the rest of the world dictate what's acceptable or unacceptable. Unbound by tradition, Alternatives make it up as they go along and don't mind if they go against prevailing patterns and norms.

Remember, we asked which category best describes the individual's attitudes *right now*. That's because we've discovered that most people's normal changes over time and circumstances (with losses or gains in income, for instance, or with the number of children). You might be Traditional right now, for example, but if you were to get divorced down the road you might revise your initial feelings about marriage and claim the Alternative category. We all reserve the right to change our ideas and our style.

Which Normal Bar category do you think describes most couples in the United States at this moment in time? The norm in the United States is still Traditional! Thirty-nine percent of our respondents (38% of women and 43% of men) believe that commitment and unconditional love define a normal, happy relationship.

But the Independents are not far behind! A full fourth of respondents (27% of women and 22% of men) see a normal relationship as important and enjoyable, but not necessarily a lifelong commitment. Then come the Undecideds at 15% (17% female and 12% male), followed by Dreamers (9% female and 12% male) and Self-sacrificers (7% female and 9% male). The smallest normal category is Alternative, a view embraced by just 3% of women and 2% of men.

Looking at these categories, which individuals do you think are most likely to be happy in their relationships? If you guessed the Traditionals, you'd be right. Eighty percent of the Traditionals said they are very happy with their partners, compared to 67% of the Independents.

And how does this line up with sexual satisfaction? The Traditionals *still* come in the highest, with 47% describing themselves as very happy. However, the Alternatives slide into a close second at 41%. The Alternatives may not be the highest in relationship happiness but that doesn't seem to hinder their ability to have extremely satisfying sex lives. This suggests a possible connection between experimentation and sexual pleasure!

And what about relationship norms in the rest of the world? The Traditional attitude remains the top category in all the countries we surveyed, and the Traditionals also are the happiest of couples internationally! That makes sense. These are the people who have made a solid commitment to the idea and practice of commitment and who venerate love, loyalty, and marriage.

Amid widespread media reports and public concern about the demise of lifelong marriage, it is something of a surprise to see that people in relationships of all types still describe their values toward relationship as traditional, at least insofar as their personal aspirations.

The Pursuit of Relationship Happiness

It's been said that life is a work in progress that can never be perfected. One reason is that everyone has his or her own vision of perfection, just as we all have our own normals. Moreover, all relationships grow, all people change, and all couples can become less—and more—intimate over time. Substantial divorce rates throughout the world attest to the difficulty of sustaining happy relationships over time, and not everyone will have a happy ending. But as the Normal Bar proves, difficult does not mean uncommon, much less impossible.

NORMALIZING THE NEW NORMAL

If your partner does something you really like, say, "I want that to be our new normal!"

We've shown that couples can make unwise choices—even denying each other the affection each person needs and wants—yet still support love and commitment. We aren't perfect and we get into bad habits, but most of us still remain attracted and committed to our partners.

It's not that complicated! The things that make the biggest difference in relationships worldwide make up a short and poignant list. Couples need to make each other their top priority; they need to make love, give affection, listen and talk, have fun, be romantic, and be respectful. Partners need to support each other and make fewer assumptions about what the other person wants, relying on conversation rather than guesswork. It's easy to mistake each other's intentions and thoughts, but with the help of a few tools, it's also easy to create a new normal that is more aware, more intimate, and more mutually satisfying.

We hope this book has given you some new insights and positive ways to relate to each other. You may be relieved and proud to see that your normal is on a path that leads to happiness. If, however, you feel that your normal is out of kilter and not bringing both of you the joy and love you want, notice that even small adjustments can put more love and understanding into your relationship. Whenever your partner does something you like and that you think might work better for both of you, say that you want this to be your NEW NORMAL!

Finally, just talking about the Normal Bar data with your partner can spark conversations that would otherwise be difficult to bring up. When you discuss our findings together, you'll learn much more about your partner and your relationship than you ever imagined. For couples with problems that need much bigger solutions, we include a number of resources at the back of this book. But remember, much of what you need—perhaps everything—can be achieved by mutually envisioning a realistic normal that the two of you truly want, then working together to make that new reality come alive and thrive. The ultimate choice about who you want to be together belongs to you.

Resources

For additional online resources, please visit our website, www.thenormalbar.com.

Berzon, Betty. *Permanent Partners: Building Gay and Lesbian Relationships that Last.* Plume, 2004.

de Bonvoisin, Ariane. *The First 30 Days: Your Guide to Any Change (and Loving Your Life More).* Harper One, 2008.

Carpenter, Laura, and John DeLamater, eds. *Sex for Life: From Virginity to Viagra, How Sexuality Changes Throughout Our Lives.* New York University Press, 2012.

Chapman, Gary. *The Five Love Languages: The Secret to Love that Lasts,* 2nd edition. Northfield Publishing, 2009.

Cherlin, Andrew. *The Marriage Go-Round: The State of Marriage and the Family in America Today.* Vintage, 2010.

Coontz, Stephanie. *Marriage, a History: How Love Conquered Marriage.* Penguin Books, 2006.

Dunas, Felice. *Passion Play: Ancient Secrets for a Lifetime of Health and Happiness Through Sensational Sex.* Riverhead Books, 1998.

Fisher, Helen. *Why We Love: The Nature and Chemistry of Romantic Love.* Henry Holt, 2004.

Gerson, Kathleen. *The Unfinished Revolution: How a New Generation Is Reshaping Family, Work, and Gender in America.* Oxford University Press, 2010.

Godek, Gregory J. P. *1001 Ways to Be Romantic.* Source Books, 2000.

Gottman, John, and Joan DeClaire. *The Relationship Cure.* Three Rivers Press, 2001.

Gottman, John, and Nan Silver. *The Seven Principles for Making*

Marriage Work: A Practical Guide from the Country's Foremost Relationship Expert. Three Rivers Press, 2000.

Gottman, John. *Why Marriages Succeed or Fail: And How You Can Make Yours Last.* Simon & Schuster, 1995.

Hendrix, Harville. *Getting the Love You Want: A Guide for Couples.* Henry Holt, 2007.

Hooper, Anne. *The Ultimate Sex Guide.* DK Publishing, Inc., 1996.

Johnson, Sue. *Hold Me Tight: Seven Conversations for a Lifetime of Love.* Little, Brown and Company, 2008.

Keesling, Barbara. *Talk Sexy to the One You Love: And Other Secrets for Improving Communication.* Harper Perennial, 1997.

Kirshenbaum, Mira. *Too Good to Leave, Too Bad to Stay: A Step-by-Step Guide to Help You Decide Whether to Stay In or Get Out of Your Relationship.* Plume, 1997.

Klein, Marty. *Sexual Intelligence: What We Really Want from Sex and How to Get It.* Harper One, 2012.

Lerner, Harriet. *The Dance of Intimacy.* William Morrow, 1990.

Lever, Janet, and Pepper Schwartz. *The Great Sex Weekend.* World Wide Romance, 2012.

McCarthy, Barry and Emily. *Getting It Right the First Time: Creating a Healthy Marriage.* Routledge, 2004.

Olsen, David. *The Couple's Survival Workbook: What You Can Do to Reconnect With Your Partner and Make Your Marriage Work.* Echo Point Books, 2011.

Orbuch, Terry. *5 Simple Steps to Take Your Marrige from Good to Great.* Delacorte Press, 2009.

Perel, Esther. *Mating in Captivity: Unlocking Erotic Intelligence.* Harper Perennial, 2007.

Pope, Tara Parker. *For Better: How the Surprising Science of Happy Couples Can Help Your Marriage Succeed.* Plume Books, 2011.

Risman, Barbara, ed. *Families as They Really Are.* Norton, 2009.

Ryan, Christopher, and Cacilda Jethá. *Sex at Dawn: How We Mate, Why We Stray, and What It Means for Modern Relationships.* Harper Perennial, 2011.

Schnarch, David. *Intimacy & Desire: Awaken the Passion in Your Relationship.* Beaufort Books, 2011.

———. *Passionate Marriage: Keeping Love and Intimacy Alive in Committed Relationships.* Norton, 2009.

Schwartz, Pepper. *Finding Your Perfect Match.* Putnam, 2006.

———. *Love Between Equals: How Peer Marriage Really Works.* Free Press, 1995.

Schwartz, Pepper, and Janet Lever. *The Getaway Guide to the Great Sex Weekend—A Proven Program by National Experts.* World Wide Romance Publication, 2012.

———. *Perfect Places for Passion and Romance at Any Age.* AARP Publications, 2013.

Stacey, Judith. *Unhitched: Love, Marriage, and Family Values from West Hollywood to Western China.* New York University Press, 2011.

APPENDIX

Methodology:

The Normal Bar *Survey*

Data for *The Normal Bar* were obtained using a unique Web-based interactive survey created specifically for this project. Initially hosted in English by the project's media partners (*Reader's Digest*, Huffington Post, AOL, and AARP), *The Normal Bar* survey was subsequently translated into Mandarin, Hungarian, and Spanish. In the project's first research phase more than 70,000 individuals worldwide contributed data, and by the book's completion the total number of respondents was expected to rise well above 100,000.

The overwhelming response to the survey is, of course, partly attributable to the topic. Questions about what's normal and how each of us compares to others are intrinsically interesting, especially when they center on romantic relationships, and this provides individuals with an incentive to participate.

But the survey's popularity also derives from its mechanics. If you've yet to take *The Normal Bar* survey and would like to, it's still available at www.thenormalbar.com. The survey was designed to be fun, as reflected in the original cartoons illustrating various subtopics. But intriguingly, the survey keeps respondents engaged and answering questions by providing a way to view how other people have answered the same questions. At the end the respondent can see how his or her responses created an overall profile of how he or she thinks.

Perhaps most important, the OnQ survey technology that was used to develop *The Normal Bar* questionnaire allows the survey to branch down distinct paths tailored to each respondent. If, for example, an individual says he or she has cheated on a current partner, then we ask for details on the topic. If the individual hasn't cheated, no other questions on that topic appear.

Apart from a set of core questions everyone was asked to answer, we divided relationship topics into sixteen areas and then created two sets of parallel topical modules for those in and out of a relationship. After moving through the core, a person selects which module he or she wants to answer, with topics ranging from Affection & Romance to Family to Health to Money to Sex. Once the person completes a given module, there is the chance to complete another—either immediately or at a later time, using a personalized link. There is a method to this madness: An individual is more likely to complete a long survey if he or she plays an active role in selecting the topics to grapple with.

The Normal Bar *Sample*

Most readers of *The Normal Bar* will be familiar with the concept of sampling. (For example, it's common to see survey results in the media based on samples of 1,000 individuals with a margin of error of +/− 3% or of 400 individuals with a margin of error of +/− 5%.) While *The Normal Bar* sample is very large, some people have pointed out that it's smaller than many poll results reported on cable news channels or large Web sites. True, but those attempts by big media platforms to take the population's pulse are typically flawed in one key respect: They ask only a *single* question. The goal of these "pulse takers" is to determine what millions of people think about a political candidate, an issue, a product—or even who can belt out the best song on *American Idol*. These one-question polls are almost always based on a diffuse aggregate of Americans. These surveys cannot tell us how our views stack up against particular subsets of society—for example, people who resemble us in age, gender, or sexual orientation.

The Normal Bar survey is the farthest thing from a one-question poll. In our most intense phase of data collection, from April 2011 through November 2011, respondents on average completed nearly 100 questions, and more than half completed at least 65 questions; 10% of respondents actually answered 170 questions or more, and one thirty-six-year-old married woman, who also worked full-time, answered 670 questions! Altogether this sample provided approximately 1.7 million answers to approximately 1,300 different questions.

So, as measured according to two key criteria—number of questions and number of respondents—*The Normal Bar* survey provides an unparalleled data resource, especially compared with other widely cited studies of people's love lives. The era of large-scale systematic study of sexual behavior began with 12,000 interviews conducted by Dr. Alfred Kinsey and his research team in the 1930s and '40s. In the 1970s, *The Hite Report on Female Sexality,* which contributed important new insights on female sexuality, was based on a sample of 4,000 women (out of a total of 100,000 questionnaires distributed) and used three different questionnaire versions, the longest of which contained only 63 questions. Other notable survey projects include a random-sample study in the 1990s of approximately 3,500 U.S. adults by researchers at the University of Chicago, and, in 2009, another random-sample study of 6,000 respondents conducted by researchers at Indiana University—both surveys mainly focused on understanding individual sex lives. Not willing to let the academics have all the fun, condom maker Durex in 2008 sponsored the Durex Sexual Wellbeing Global Survey, which was completed by 26,000 adults in twenty-six countries.

Crucially, *The Normal Bar* survey is different from these other studies because it examines many aspects of relationship behavior *in addition to* sexual activity.

In *The Normal Bar* you see percentages; and we talk extensively about differences in attitudes, behaviors, and beliefs between groups. In such instances, we're reporting on the clear differences or lack of differences we see in our sample. But understand: We can't use these data to definitively indicate differences in the general population. All of our conclusions are based on what we've gathered from those who've answered our queries. Still, in many cases, our results are consistent with larger population studies; so, in those cases, we mention the results with an even greater degree of confidence.

It's also worth pointing out that random samples have become what could be called a gold standard based on copper. More orthodox polls today are showing decreasing response rates and a mixed bag of methods, in large part because access to potential respondents via landlines, cell phones, or the Internet has become more difficult. True random samples are becoming increasingly elusive. It is progressively more difficult to say just what population a sample represents.

In the table below, we see that members of *The Normal Bar* sample differ in important ways from the U.S. population as measured by the Bureau of the Census. *Normal Bar* participants are more likely to be women, are younger, are more likely to be white, are less likely to be Hispanic, and are more likely to have higher levels of education than the U.S. population overall. This is not an uncommon sampling issue—after all, certain kinds of people are more likely to be drawn to questionnaires and polls.

THE NORMAL BAR SAMPLE COMPARED TO THE
U.S. ADULT POPULATION

	U.S. Census 2010	The Normal Bar
Gender		
Male	48.5%	32.1%
Female	51.5%	67.9%
Age		
18 to 24	13.0%	16.6%
25 to 34	17.5%	27.4%
35 to 44	17.5%	20.0%
45 to 54	19.2%	19.3%
55 and older	32.8%	16.7%
Race/ethnicity		
White	72.4%	88.9%
Non-white	27.6%	11.1%
Hispanic	16.3%	6.4%
Non-Hispanic	83.7%	93.6%
Education (age 25 or older)		
No college degree	64.3%	36.0%
Associate's or bachelor's degree	25.3%	37.0%
Graduate or professional degree	10.4%	27.0%

Sampling issues are the reason why most of *The Normal Bar* results are reported as they relate to specific demographic groups. While our sample may contain disproportionately higher or lower percentages of certain groups, this fact is less of an issue when we talk about the findings within that group.

This brings us to a final important methodological point. Even within a particular demographic subgroup—let's say, married women between the ages of 35 and 44 with a bachelor's degree—there will be other important differences between our sample and the general population. Remember, we mentioned earlier that interest in topic is a strong predictor of participation in a survey. It's safe to assume that married women between the ages of 35 and 44 with a bachelor's degree who took *The Normal Bar* survey are more interested in the quality of their relationships than are similar women in the United States who chose not to participate in the study.

So is this potential bias a problem? We don't think so. You may have noticed that surveys about elections are often based on samples of "likely" voters; ever wondered why? If you want to predict the outcome of an election, you're most interested in surveying those who are likely to vote. If *The Normal Bar* survey sample contains people who are especially interested in the quality of their relationships, that's not a problem—rather, it's a good thing. It simply means that *The Normal Bar* respondents are like you.

About the Authors

CHRISANNA NORTHRUP created *The Normal Bar* project and is the CEO of YOU Got Challenged! Inc., a customized online program that motivates people to change their normal to a healthier one.

PEPPER SCHWARTZ received her PhD in sociology from Yale University, and is a professor of sociology at the University of Washington and the author of sixteen books.

JAMES WITTE, a Harvard PhD, is a professor of sociology and director of the Center for Social Science Research at George Mason University.

To find out more about *The Normal Bar* and its authors, go to www.thenormalbar.com.